A Man's Value to Society

by Newell Dwight Hillis

TO MY WIFE

CONTENTS

THE ELEMENTS OF WORTH IN THE INDIVIDUAL

"There is nothing that makes men rich and strong but that which they carry inside of them. Wealth is of the heart, not of the hand."--John Milton.

"Until we know why the rose is sweet or the dew drop pure, or the rainbow beautiful, we cannot know why the poet is the best benefactor of society. The soldier fights for his native land, but the poet touches that land with the charm that makes it worth fighting for and fires the warrior's heart with energy invincible. The statesman enlarges and orders liberty in the state, but the poet fosters the core of liberty in the heart of the citizen. The inventor multiplies the facilities of life, but the poet makes life better worth living."-- George Wm. Curtis.

"Not all men are of equal value. Not many Platos: only one, to whom a thousand lesser minds look up and learn to think. Not many Dantes: one, and a thousand poets tune their harps to his and repeat his notes. Not many Raphaels: one, and no second. But a thousand lesser artists looking up to him are lifted to his level. Not many royal hearts--great magazines of kindness. Happy the town blessed with a few great minds and a few great hearts. One such citizen will civilize an entire community."--H.

I

THE ELEMENTS OF WORTH IN THE INDIVIDUAL

Our scientific experts are investigating the wastes of society. Their reports indicate that man is a great spendthrift. He seems not so much a husbandman, making the most of the treasures of his life-garden, as a robber looting a storehouse for booty.

Travelers affirm that one part of the northern pineries has been wasted by man's careless fires and much of the rest by his reckless axe. Coal experts insist that a large percentage of heat passes out of the chimney. The new chemistry claims that not a little of the precious ore is cast upon the slag heap.

In the fields the farmers overlook some ears of corn and pass by some handfuls of wheat. In the work-room the scissors leave selvage and remnant.

In the mill the saw and plane refuse slabs and edges. In the kitchen a part of what the husband carries in, the wife's wasteful cooking casts out. But the secondary wastes involve still heavier losses. Man's carelessness in the factory breaks delicate machinery, his ignorance spoils raw materials, his idleness burns out boilers, his recklessness blows up engines; and no skill of manager in juggling figures in January can retrieve the wastes of June.

Passing through the country the traveler finds the plow rusting in the furrow, mowers and reapers exposed to rain and snow; passing through the city he sees the docks lined with boats, the alleys full of broken vehicles, while the streets exhibit some broken-down men. A journey through life is like a journey along the trackway of a retreating army; here a valuable ammunition wagon is abandoned because a careless smith left a flaw in the tire; there a brass cannon is deserted because a tug was improperly stitched; yonder a brave soldier lies dying in the thicket where he fell because excited men forgot the use of an ambulance. What with the wastes of intemperance and ignorance, of idleness and class wars, the losses of society are enormous. But man's prodigality with his material treasures does but interpret his wastefulness of the greater riches of mind and heart. Life's chief destructions are in the city of man's soul. Many persons seem to be trying to solve this problem: "Given a soul stored with great treasure, and three score and ten years for happiness and usefulness, how shall one kill the time and waste the treasure?" Man's pride over his casket stored with gems must be modified by the reflection that daily his pearls are cast before swine, that should have been woven into coronets.

Man's evident failure to make the most out of his material life suggests a study of the elements in each citizen that make him of value to his age and community. What are the measurements of mankind, and why is it that daily some add new treasures to the storehouse of civilization, while others take from and waste the store already accumulated? These are questions of vital import. Many and varied estimates of man's value have been made. Statisticians reckon the average man's value at $600 a year. Each worker in wood, iron or brass stands for an engine or industrial plant worth $10,000, producing at 6 per cent. an income of $600. The death of the average workman, therefore, is equivalent to the destruction of a $10,000 mill or engine. The economic loss through the non-productivity of 20,000 drunkards is equal to one Chicago fire involving two hundred millions. Of course, some men produce less and others more than $600 a year; and some there are who have no industrial value--non-producers, according to Adam Smith; paupers, according to John Stuart Mill; thieves, according to Paul, who says, "Let him that stole steal no more, but rather work." In this group let us include the tramps, who hold that the world owes them a living; these are they who fail to realize that society has given them support through infancy and childhood; has given them language, literature, liberty. Wise men know that the noblest and strongest have received from society a thousandfold more than they can ever repay, though they vex all the days and nights with ceaseless toil. In this number of non-sufficing persons are to be included the paupers--paupers plebeian, supported in the poorhouse by many citizens; paupers patrician, supported in palace by one citizen, generally father or ancestor; the two classes differing in that one is the foam at the top of the glass and the other the dregs at the bottom. To these two groups let us add the social parasites, represented by thieves, drunkards, and persons of the baser sort whose business it is to trade in human passion. We revolt from the red aphides upon the plant, the caterpillar upon the tree, the vermin upon bird or beast. How much more do we revolt from those human vermin whose business it is to propagate parasites upon the body politic! The condemnation of life is that a man consumes more than he produces, taking out of society's granary that which other hands have put in. The praise of life is that one is self-sufficing, taking less out than he put into the storehouse of civilization.

A man's original capital comes through his ancestry. Nature invests the grandsire's ability, and compounds it for the grandson. Plato says: "The child is a charioteer driving two steeds up the long life-hill; one steed is white, representing our best impulses; one steed is dark, standing for our worst passions." Who gave these steeds their color? Our fathers, Plato replies, and the child may not change one hair, white or black. Oliver Wendell Holmes would have us think that a man's value is determined a hundred years before his birth. The ancestral ground slopes upward toward the mountain-minded man. The great never appear suddenly. Seven generations of clergymen make ready for Emerson, each a signboard pointing to the coming philosopher. The Mississippi has power to bear up fleets for war or peace because the storms of a thousand summers and the snows of a thousand winters have lent depth and power. The measure of greatness in a man is determined by the intellectual streams and moral tides flowing down from the ancestral hills and emptying into the human soul. The Bach family included one hundred and twenty musicians. Paganini was born with muscles in his wrists like whipcords. What was unique in Socrates was first unique in Sophroniscus. John ran before Jesus, but Zacharias foretold John. No electricity along rope wires, and no vital living truths along rope nerves to spongy brain. There are millions in our world who have been rendered physical and moral paupers by the sins of their ancestors. Their forefathers doomed them to be hewers of wood and drawers of water. A century must pass before one of their children can crowd his way up and show strength enough to shape a tool, outline a code, create an industry, reform a wrong. Despotic governments have stunted men--made them thin-blooded and low-browed, all backhead and no forehead. Each child has been likened to a cask whose staves represent trees growing on hills distant and widely separated; some staves are sound and solid, standing for right-living ancestors; some are worm eaten, standing for ancestors whose integrity was consumed by vices. At birth all the staves are brought together in the infant cask--empty, but to be filled by parents and teachers and friends. As the waste-barrel in the alley is filled with refuse and filth, so the orphan waifs in our streets are made receptacles of all vicious thoughts and deeds. These children are not so much born as damned into life. But how different is the childhood of some others. On the Easter day, in foreign cathedrals, a beauteous vase is placed beside the altar, and as the multitudes crowd forward and the solemn procession moves up the aisles, men and women cast into the vase their gifts of gold and silver and pearls and lace and rich textures. The well-born child seems to be such a vase, unspeakably beautiful, filled with knowledges and integrities more precious than gold and pearls. "Let him who would be great select the right parents," was the keen dictum of President Dwight.

By the influence of the racial element, the laborer in northern Europe, viewed as a producing machine, doubles the industrial output of his southern brother. The child of the tropics is out of the race. For centuries he has dozed under the banana tree, awakening only to shake the tree and bring down ripe fruit for his hunger, eating to sleep again. His muscles are flabby, his blood is thin, his brain unequal to the strain of two ideas in one day. When Sir John Lubbock had fed the chief in the South Sea Islands he began to ask him questions, but within ten minutes the savage was sound asleep. When awakened the old chief said: "Ideas make me so sleepy." Similarly, the warm Venetian blood has given few great men to civilization; but the hills of Scotland and New England produce scholars, statesmen, poets, financiers, with the alacrity with which Texas produces cotton or Missouri corn. History traces certain influential nations back to a single progenitor of unique strength of body and character. Thus Abraham, Theseus, and Cadmus seem like springs feeding great and increasing rivers. One wise and original thinker founds a tribe, shapes the destiny of a nation, and multiplies himself in the lives of future millions. In accordance with this law, tenacity reappears in every Scotchman; wit sparkles in every Irishman; vivacity is in every Frenchman's blood; the Saxon is a colonizer and originates institutions. During the construction of the Suez Canal it was discovered that workmen with veins filled with Teutonic blood had a commercial value two and a half times greater than the Egyptians. Similarly, during the Indian war, the Highland troops endured double the strain of the native forces. Napoleon shortened the stature of the French people two inches by choosing all the taller of his 30,000,000 subjects and killing them in war. Waxing indignant, Horace Mann thinks "the forehead of the Irish peasantry was lowered an inch when the government made it an offense punishable with fine, imprisonment, and a traitor's death to be the teacher of children." A wicked government can make agony, epidemic, brutalize a race, and reaching forward, fetter generations yet unborn. "Blood tells," says science. But blood is the radical element put out at compound interest and handed forward to generations yet unborn.

The second measure of a man's value to society is found in his original endowment of physical strength. The child's birth-stock of vital force is his capital to be traded upon. Other things being equal his productive value is to be estimated mathematically upon the basis of physique. Born weak and nerveless, he must go to society's ambulance wagon, and so impede the onward march. Born vigorous and rugged, he can help to clear the forest roadway or lead the advancing columns. Fundamentally man is a muscular machine for producing the ideas that shape conduct and character. All fine thinking stands with one foot on fine brain fiber. Given large physical organs, lungs with capacity sufficient to oxygenate the life-currents as they pass upward; large arteries through which the blood may have full course, run, and be glorified; a brain healthy and balanced with a compact nervous system, and you have the basis for computing what will be a man's value to society. Men differ, of course, in ways many--they differ in the number and range of their affections, in the scope of conscience, in taste and imagination, and in moral energy. But the original point of variance is physical. Some have a small body and a powerful mind, like a Corliss engine in a tiny boat, whose frail structure will soon be racked to pieces. Others are born with large bodies and very little mind, as if a toy engine were set to run a mudscow. This means that the poor engineer must pole up stream all his life. Others, by ignorance of parent, or accident through nurse, or through their own blunder or sin, destroy their bodily capital. Soon they are like boats cast high and dry upon the beach, doomed to sun-cracking and decay. Then, in addition to these absolute weaknesses, come the disproportions of the body, the distemperature of various organs. It is not necessary for spoiling a timepiece to break its every bearing; one loose screw stops all the wheels. Thus a very slight error as to the management of the bodily mechanism is sufficient to prevent fine creative work as author, speaker, or inventor. Few men, perhaps, ever learn how to so manage their brain and stomach as to be capable of high-pressure brain action for days at a time--until the cumulative mental forces break through all obstacles and conquer success. A great leader represents a kind of essence of common sense, but rugged common sense is sanity of nerve and brain. He who rules and leads must have mind and will, but he must have chest and stomach also. Beecher says the gun carriage must be in proportion to the gun it carries. When health goes the gun is spiked. Ideas are arrows, and the body is the bow that sends them home. The mind aims; the body fires.

Good health may be better than genius or wealth or honor. It was when the gymnasium had made each Athenian youth an Apollo in health and strength that the feet of the Greek race ran most nimbly along the paths of art and literature and philosophy.

Another test of a man's value is an intellectual one. The largest wastes of any nation are through ignorance. Failure is want of knowledge; success is knowing how. Wealth is not in things of iron, wood and stone. Wealth is in the brain that organizes the metal. Pig iron is worth $20 a ton; made into horse shoes, $90; into knife blades, $200; into watch springs, $1,000. That is, raw iron $20, brain power, $980. Millet bought a yard of canvas for 1 franc, paid 2 more francs for a hair brush and some colors; upon this canvas he spread his genius, giving us "The Angelus." The original investment in raw material was 60 cents; his intelligence gave that raw material a value of $105,000. One of the pictures at the World's Fair represented a savage standing on the bank of a stream, anxious but ignorant as to how he could cross the flood. Knowledge toward the metal at his feet gave the savage an axe; knowledge toward the tree gave him a canoe; knowledge toward the union of canoes gave him a boat; knowledge toward the wind added sails; knowledge toward fire and water gave him the ocean steamer. Now, if from the captain standing on the prow of that floating palace, the City of New York, we could take away man's knowledge as we remove peel after peel from an onion, we would have from the iron steamer, first, a sailboat, then a canoe, then axe and tree, and at last a savage, naked and helpless to cross a little stream. In the final analysis it is ignorance that wastes; it is knowledge that saves; it is wisdom that gives precedence. If sleep is the brother of death, ignorance is full brother to both sleep and death. An untaught faculty is at once quiescent and dead. An ignorant man has been defined as one "whom God has packed up and men have not unfolded. The best forces in such a one are perpetually paralyzed. Eyes he has, but he cannot see the length of his hand; ears he has, and all the finest sounds in creation escape him; a tongue he has, and it is forever blundering." A mechanic who has a chest of forty tools and can use only the hammer, saw, and gimlet, has little chance with his fellows and soon falls far behind. An educated mind is one fully awakened to all the sights and scenes and forces in the world through which he moves. This does not mean that a $2,000 man can be made out of a two-cent boy by sending him to college. Education is mind-husbandry; it changes the size but not the sort. But if no amount of drill will make a Shetland pony show a two-minute gait, neither will the thoroughbred show this speed save through long and assiduous and patient education. The primary fountains of our Nation's wealth are not in fields and forests and mines, but in the free schools, churches, and printing presses. Ignorance breeds misery, vice, and crime. Mephistopheles was a cultured devil, but he is the exception. History knows no illiterate seer or sage or saint. No Dante or Shakespeare ever had to make "his X mark."

When John Cabot Lodge made his study of the distribution of ability in the United States, he found that in ninety years five of the great Western States had produced but twenty-seven men who were mentioned in the American and English encyclopedias, while little Massachusetts had 2,686 authors, orators, philosophers, and builders of States. But analysis shows that the variance is one of education and ideas. Boston differs from Quebec as differ their methods of instruction. The New England settlers were Oxford and Cambridge men that represented the best blood, brain, and accumulated culture of old England. Landing in the forest they clustered their cabins around the building that was at once church, school, library, and town hall. Rising early and sitting up late they plied their youth with ideas of liberty and intelligence. They came together on Sunday morning at nine o'clock to listen to a prayer one hour long, a sermon of three hours, and after a cold lunch heard a second brief sermon of two hours and a half--those who did not die became great. What Sunday began the week continued. We may smile at their methods but we must admire the men they produced. Mark the intellectual history of Northampton. During its history this town has sent out 114 lawyers, 112 ministers, 95 physicians, 100 educators, 7 college presidents, 30 professors, 24 editors, 6 historians, 14 authors, among whom are George Bancroft, John Lothrop Motley, Professor Whitney, the late J.G. Holland; 38 officers of State, 28 officers of the United States, including members of the Senate, and one President.[1] How comes it that this little colony has raised up this great company of authors, statesmen, reformers? No mere chance is working here. The relation between sunshine and harvest is not more essential than the relation between these folk and their renowned descendants. Fruit after his kind is the divine explanation of Northampton's influence upon the nation. "Education makes men great" is the divine dictum. George William Curtis has said: "The Revolutionary leaders were all trained men, as the world's leaders always have been from the day when Themistocles led the educated Athenians at Salamis, to that when Von Moltke marshaled the educated Germans against France. The sure foundations of states are laid in knowledge, not in ignorance; and every sneer at education, at book learning, which is the recorded wisdom of the experience of mankind, is the demagogue's sneer at intelligent liberty, inviting national degeneration and ruin."

Consider, also, how the misfits of life affect man's value. The successful man grasps the handle of his being. He moves in the line of least resistance. That one accomplishes most whose heart sings while his hand works. Like animals men have varied uses. The lark sings, the ox bears burdens, the horse is for strength and speed. But men who are wise toward beasts are often foolish toward themselves. Multitudes drag themselves toward the factory or field who would have moved toward the forum with "feet as hind's feet." Other multitudes fret and chafe in the office whose desires are in the streets and fields. Whoever scourges himself to a task he hates serves a hard master, and the slave will get but scant pay. If a farmer should hitch horses to a telescope and try to plow with it he would ruin the instrument in the summer and starve his family in the winter. Not the wishes of parent, nor the vanity of wife, nor the pride of place, but God and nature choose occupation. Each child is unique, as new as was the first arrival upon this planet. The school is to help the boy unpack what intellectual tools he has; education does not change, but puts temper into these tools. No man can alter his temperament, though trying to he can break his heart. How pathetic the wrecks of men who have chosen the wrong occupation! The driver bathes the raw shoulder of a horse whose collar does not fit, but when men make their misfits and the heart is sore society does not soothe, but with whips it scourges the man to his fruitless task. This large class may be counted unproductive. John Stuart Mill placed the industrial mismatings among the heavier losses of society.

To this element of wisdom in relating one's self to duties must be added skill in maintaining smooth relations with one's fellows. Men may produce much by industry and ability, and yet destroy more by the malign elements they carry. The proud domineering employer tears down with one hand what he builds up with the other. One foolish man can cost a city untold treasure. How many factories have failed because the owner has no skill in managing men and mollifying difficulties. History shows that stupid thrones and wars go together, while skillful kings bring long intervals of peace. Contrasting the methods of two prominent men, an editor once said: "The first man in making one million cost society ten millions; but the other so produced his one million as to add ten more to society's wealth." A most disastrous strike in England's history had its origin in ignorance of this principle. The miners of a certain coal field had suffered a severe cut in wages. They had determined to accept it, though it took their children out of school, and took away their meat dinner. When the hour appointed for the conference came, prudence would have dictated that every cause of irritation be guarded against. But the employer foolishly drove his liveried carriage into the center of the vast crowd of workmen, and for an hour flaunted his wealth before the sore-hearted miners. When the men saw the footman, the prancing horses, the gold-plated harness, and thought of their starving wives, they reversed their acceptance of the cut in wages. They plunged into a long strike, taking this for their motto: "Furs for his footmen and gold plate for his horses, and also three meals a day for our wives and children." Now, the ensuing strike and riots, long protracted, cost England ?,000,000. But that bitter strike was all needless. These are the men who take off the chariot wheels for God's advancing hosts. When one comes to the front who has skill in allaying friction, all society begins a new forward march. Skill in personal carriage has much to do with a man's value.

Integrity enhances human worth. Iniquities devastate a city like fire and pestilence. Social wealth and happiness are through right living. Goodness is a commodity. Conscience in a cashier has a cash value. If arts and industries are flowers and fruits, moralities are the roots that nourish them. Disobedience is slavery. Obedience is liberty. Disobedience to law of fire or water or acid is death. Obedience to law of color gives the artist his skill; obedience to the law of eloquence gives the orator his force; obedience to the law of iron gives the inventor his tool; disobedience to the law of morals gives waste and want and wretchedness. That individual or nation is hastening toward poverty that does not love the right and hate the wrong. So certain is the penalty of wrongdoing that sin seems infinitely stupid. Every transgression is like an iron plate thrown into the air; gravity will pull it back upon the wrongdoer's head to wound him. It has been said for a man to betray his trust for money, is for him to stand on the same intellectual level with a monkey that scalds its throat with boiling water because it is thirsty. A drunkard is one who exchanges ambrosia and nectar for garbage. A profligate is one who declines an invitation to banquet with the gods that he may dine out of an ash barrel. What blight is to the vine, sin is to a man. When the first thief appeared in Plymouth colony a man was withdrawn from the fields to make locks for the houses; when two thieves came a second toiler was withdrawn from the factory to serve as night watchman. Soon others were taken from productive industry to build a jail and to interpret and execute the law. Every sin costs the state much hard cash. Consider what wastes hatred hath wrought. Once Italy and Greece and Central Europe made one vast storehouse filled with precious art treasures. But men turned the cathedrals into arsenals of war. If the clerks in some porcelain or cut-glass store should attend to their duties in the morning, and each afternoon have a pitched battle, during which they should throw the vases and cups and medallions at each other, and each night pick up a piece of vase, here an armless Venus and there a headless Apollo, to put away for future generations to study, we should have that which answers precisely to what has gone on for centuries through hatreds and class wars. An outlook upon society is much like a visit to Lisbon after an earthquake has filled the streets with debris and shaken down homes, palaces, and temples. History is full of the ruins of cities and empires. Not time, but disobedience, hath wrought their destruction. New civilizations will be reared by coming generations; uprightness will lay the foundations and integrity will complete the structure. The temple is righteousness in which God dwelleth.

"Have life more abundantly." Man is not fated to a scant allowance nor a fixed amount, but he is allured forward by an unmeasured possibility. Personality may be enlarged and enriched. It has been said that Cromwell was the best thing England ever produced. And the mission of Jesus Christ is to carry each up from littleness to full-orbed largeness. It has always been true that when some genius, e.g., Watt, invents a model the people have reproduced it times innumerable. So what man asks for is not the increase of birth talent, but a pattern after which this raw material can be fashioned. Carbon makes charcoal, and carbon makes diamond, too, but the "sea of light" is carbon crystallized to a pattern. Builders lay bricks by plan; the musician follows his score; the value of a York minster is not in the number of cords of stone, but in the plan that organized them; and the value of a man is in the reply to this question: Have the raw materials of nature been wrought up into unity and harmony by the Exemplar of human life? Daily he is here to stir the mind with holy ambitions; to wing the heart with noble aspirations; to inspire with an all-conquering courage; to vitalize the whole manhood. By making the individual rich within he creates value without. For all things are first thoughts. Tools, fabrics, ships, houses, books are first ideas, afterward crystallized into outer form. A great picture is a beautiful conception rushing into visible expression upon the canvas. Wake up taste in a man and he beautifies his home. Wake up conscience and he drives iniquities out of his heart. Wake up his ideas of freedom and he fashions new laws. Jesus Christ is here to inflame man's soul within that he may transform and enrich his life without. No picture ever painted, no statue ever carved, no cathedral ever builded is half so beautiful as the Christ-formed man. What is man's value to society? Let him who knoweth what is in us reply: "What shall it profit a man if he gain the whole world and lose his own soul?"

FOOTNOTES:

[1] Northampton Antiquities. Clark.

CHARACTER: ITS MATERIALS AND EXTERNAL TEACHERS

"Character is more than intellect. A great soul will be strong to live, as well as to think. Goodness outshines genius, as the sun makes the electric light cast a shadow."--Emerson.

"What the superior man seeks is in himself; what the small man seeks is in others."--Confucius.

"After all, the kind of world one carries about in one's self is the important thing, and the world outside takes all its grace, color and value from that."--James Russell Lowell.

"Sow an act and you reap a habit; sow a habit and you reap a character; sow a character and you reap a destiny."--Anon.

"So teach us to number our days that we may apply our hearts unto wisdom."--Psalm 90.

II

CHARACTER: ITS MATERIALS AND EXTERNAL TEACHERS

Dying, Horace Greeley exclaimed: "Fame is a vapor, popularity an accident, riches take wings, those who cheer to-day will curse to-morrow, only one thing endures--character!" These weighty words bid all remember that life's one task is the making of manhood. Our world is a college, events are teachers, happiness is the graduating point, character is the diploma God gives man. The forces that increase happiness are many, including money, friends, position; but one thing alone is indispensable to success--personal worth and manhood. He who stands forth clothed with real weight of goodness can neither be feeble in life, nor forgotten in death. Society admires its scholar, but society reveres and loves its hero whose intellect is clothed with goodness. For character is not of the intellect, but of the disposition. Its qualities strike through and color the mind and heart even as summer strikes the matured fruit through with juicy ripeness.

Of that noble Greek who governed his city by unwritten laws, the people said: "Phocion's character is more than the constitution." The weight of goodness in Lamartine was such that during the bloody days in Paris his doors were unlocked. Character in him was a defense beyond the force of rock walls or armed regiments. Emerson says there was a certain power in Lincoln, Washington and Burke not to be explained by their printed words. Burke the man was inexpressibly finer than anything he said. As a spring is more than the cup it fills, as a poet or architect is more than the songs he sings or the temple he rears, so the man is more than the book or business he fashions. Earth holds many wondrous scenes called temples, battle-fields, cathedrals, but earth holds no scene comparable for majesty and beauty to a man clothed indeed with intellect, but adorned also with integrities and virtues. Beholding such a one, well did Milton exclaim: "A good man is the ripe fruit our earth holds up to God."

Character has been defined as the joint product of nature and nurture. Nature gives the raw material, character is the carved statue. The raw material includes the racial endowment, temperament, degree of vital force, mentality, aptitude for tool or industry, for art or science. These birth-gifts are quantities, fixed and unalterable. No heart-rendings can change the two-talent nature into a ten-talent man. No agony of effort can add a cubit to the stature. The eagle flies over the chasm as easily as an ant crawls over the crack in the ground. Shakespeare writes Hamlet as easily as Tupper wrote his tales. Once an oak, always an oak. Care and culture can thicken the girth of the tree, but no degree of culture can cause an oak bough to bring forth figs instead of acorns. Rebellion against temperament and circumstance is sure to end in the breaking of the heart. Happiness and success begin with the sincere acceptance of the birth-gift and career God hath chosen.

Since no man can do his best work save as he uses his strongest faculties, the first duty of each is to search out the line of least resistance. He who has a genius for moral themes but has harnessed himself to the plow or the forge, is in danger of wrecking both happiness and character. All such misfits are fatal. No farmer harnesses a fawn to the plow, or puts an ox into the speeding-wagon. Life's problem is to make a right inventory of the gifts one carries. As no carpenter knows what tools are in the box until he lifts the lid and unwraps one shining instrument after another, so the instruments in the soul must be unfolded by education. Ours is a world where the inventor accompanies the machine with a chart, illustrating the use of each wheel and escapement. But no babe lying in the cradle ever brought with it a hand-book setting forth its mental equipment and pointing out its aptitude for this occupation, or that art or industry. The gardener plants a root with perfect certainty that a rose will come up, but no man is a prophet wise enough to tell whether this babe will unfold into quality of thinker or doer or dreamer. To each Nature whispers: "Unsight, unseen, hold fast what you have." For the soul is shadowless and mysterious. No hand can carve its outline, no brush portray its lineaments. Even the mother embosoming its infancy and carrying its weaknesses, studying it by day and night through years, sees not, she cannot see, knows not, she cannot know, into what splendor of maturity the child will unfold.

Man beholds his fellows as one beholds a volume written in a foreign language; the outer binding is seen, the inner contents are unread. Within general lines phrenology and physiognomy are helpful, but it is easier to determine what kind of a man lives in the house by looking at the knob on his front door than to determine the brain and heart within by studying the bumps upon face and forehead. Nature's dictum is, "Grasp the handle of your own being." Each must fashion his own character. Nature gives trees, but not tools; forests, but not furniture. Thus nature furnishes man with the birth materials and environment; man must work up these materials into those qualities called industry, integrity, honor, truth and love, ever patterning after that ideal man, Jesus Christ.

The influences shaping nature's raw material into character are many and various. Of old, the seer likened the soul unto clay. The mud falls upon the board before the potter, a rude mass, without form or comeliness. But an hour afterwards the clay stands forth adorned with all the beauty of a lovely vase. Thus the soul begins, a mere mass of mind, but hands many and powerful soon shape it into the outlines of some noble man or woman. These sculptors of character include home, friendship, occupation, travel, success, love, grief and death.

Life's first teacher is the external world, with its laws. Man begins at zero. The child thrusts his finger into the fire and is burned; thenceforth he learns to restrain himself in the presence of fire, and makes the flames smite the vapor for driving train or ship. The child errs in handling the sharp tool, and cuts himself; thenceforth he lifts up the axe upon the tree. The child mistakes the weight of stone, or the height of stair, and, falling, hard knocks teach him the nature and use of gravity. Daily the thorns that pierce his feet drive him back into the smooth pathway of nature's laws. The sharp pains that follow each excess teach him the pleasures of sound and right living. Nor is there one infraction of law that is not followed by pain. As sharp guards are placed at the side of the bridge over the chasm to hold men back from the abyss, so nature's laws are planted on either side of the way of life to prick and scourge erring feet back into the divine way. At length through much smiting of the body nature forces the youth into a knowledge of the world in which he lives. Man learns to carry himself safely within forests, over rivers, through fires, midst winds and storms. Soon every force in nature stands forth his willing servant; becoming like unto the steeds of the plains, that once were wild, but now are trained, and lend all their strength and force to man's loins and limbs.

Having mastered the realm of physical law, the youth is thrust into the realm of laws domestic and social. He runs up against his mates and friends, often overstepping his own rights and infringing the rights of others. Then some stronger arm falls on his, and drives him back into his own territory. Occasional chastisement through the parent and teacher, friend or enemy, reveal to him the nature of selfishness, and compel the recognition of others. Thus, through long apprenticeship, the youth finds out the laws that fence him round, that press upon him at every pore, by day and by night, in workshop or in store, at home or abroad. Slowly these laws mature manhood. When ideas are thrust into raw iron, the iron becomes a loom or an engine. Thus when God's laws are incarnated in a babe, the child is changed into the likeness of a citizen, a sage or seer. Nature, with her laws, is not only the earliest, but also the most powerful, of life's instructors.

Temptation is another teacher. Protection gives innocence, but practice gives virtue. For ship timber we pass by the sheltered hothouse, seeking the oak on the storm-swept hills. In that beautiful story of the lost paradise, God pulls down the hedge built around Adam and Eve. The government through a fence outside was succeeded by self-government inside. The hermit and the cloistered saint end their career with innocence. But Christ, struggling unto blood against sin, ends His career with character. God educates man by giving him complete charge over himself and setting him on "the barebacked horse of his own will," leaving him to break it by his own strength. Travelers to Alaska tell us that the wild berries attain a sweetness there of which our temperate clime knows nothing. Scientists say that the glowworm keeps its enemies at bay by the brightness of its own light. Man, by his love of truth and right, becomes his own castle and fortress. Cities no longer depend upon night-watchmen to guard against marauders and burglars. Once men trusted to safes and iron bars upon the windows. Now bankers ask electric lights to guard their treasure vaults.

For centuries Spain's paternal laws have compelled each Spaniard to ask his church what to think and believe. This method has robbed that people of enduring and self-reliant manhood, and made them a race of weaklings. For over-protection is a peril. Strength comes by wrestling, knowledge by observing, wisdom by thinking, and character by enduring and struggling. Exposure is often good fortune. Every Luther and Cromwell has been tempted and tempered against the day of danger and battle. As the victorious Old Guard were honored in proportion to the number and severity of the wars through which they had passed, so the temptations that seek man's destruction, when conquered, cover him with glory. Ruskin notes that the art epochs have also been epochs of war, upheaval, and tyranny. He accounts for this by saying that when tyranny was hardest, crime blackest, sin ugliest, then, in the recoil and conflict, beauty and heroism attained their highest development.

Studying the rise of the Dutch republic, Motley notes how the shocks and fiery baptisms of war changed those peasants into patriots. This explains society's enthusiasm for its hero, all scarred and gray. We admire the child's innocence, but it lacks ripeness and maturity; it is only a handful of germs. But every heart kindles and glows when the true hero stands forth in the person of some Paul or Savonarola, some Luther or Lincoln, having passed through fire, through flood, through all the thunder of life's battle, ever ripening, sweetening and enlarging, his fineness and gentleness being the result of great strength and great wisdom, accumulated through long life, until he stands, at the end of his career, as the sun stands on a summer afternoon just before it goes down. All statues and pictures become tawdry in comparison with such a rich, ripe, glowing, and glorious heart, clothed with Christlike character.

Life's teachers also includes newness and zest. First, man lives his life in fresh personal experiences. Then, by observation, he repeats his life in the career of his children. A third time he journeys around the circle, reexperiencing life in that of his grandchildren. Then, because the newness has passed away and events no longer stimulate his mind, death withdraws man from the scene and enters him in a new school. Vast is the educational value therefore attaching to the newness of life. God is so rich that no day or scene need repeat a former one. The proverb, "We never look upon the same river," tells us that all things are ever changing, and clothes each day with fresh fascination. "Whilst I read the poets," said Emerson, "I think that nothing new can be said about morning and evening; but when I see the day break I am not reminded of the Homeric and Chaucerian pictures. I am cheered by the moist, warm, glittering, budding, melodious hour that breaks down the narrow walls of my soul, and extends its life and pulsations to the very horizon."

Thus, each new day is a new continent to be explored. Each youth is a new creature, full of delightful and mysterious possibilities. Each brain comes clothed with its own secret, having its own orbit, attaining its own unique experience. Ours is a world in which each individual, each country, each age, each day, has a history peculiarly its own. This newness is a perpetual stimulant to curiosity and study. Gladstone's recipe for never growing old is, "Search out some topic in nature or life in which you have never hitherto been interested, and experience its fascinations." For some, once a picture or book has been seen, the pleasure ceases. Delight dies with familiarity. Such persons look back to the days of childhood as to the days of wonder and happiness. But the man of real vision ever beholds each rock, each herb and flower with the big eyes of children, and with a mind of perpetual wonder. For him the seed is a fountain gushing with new delights. Every youth should repeat the experience of John Ruskin.[2] Such was the enthusiasm that this author felt for God's world, that when he approached some distant mountain or saw the crags hanging over the waters, or the clouds marching through the sky, "a shiver of fear, mingled with awe," set him quivering with joy--such joy as the artist pupil feels in the presence of his noble master, such a kindling of mind and heart as Dante felt on approaching his Beatrice. Phillips Brooks grew happier as he grew older, and at fifty-seven he said: "Life seems a feast in which God keeps the best wine until the last." Up to the very end the great preacher grew by leaps and bounds, because he never lost that enthusiasm for life that makes zest and newness among life's best teachers.

By a strange paradox men are taught by monotony as well as by newness.

Ours is a world where the words, "Blessed be drudgery," are full of meaning. Culture and character come not through consuming excitements nor the whirl of pleasures. The granary is filled, not by the thunderous forces that appeal to the eye and ear, but by the secret, invisible agents; the silent energies, the mighty monarchs hidden in roots and in seeds. What rioting storms cannot do is done by the silent sap and sunshine. All the fundamental qualities called patience, perseverance, courage, fidelity, are the gains of drudgery. Character comes with commonplaces. Greatness is through tasks that have become insipid, and by duties that are irksome. The treadmill is a divine teacher. He who shovels sand year in and year out needs not our pity, for the proverb is "Every man has his own sand heap." The greatest mind, fulfilling its career, once the freshness has worn off, pursues a hackneyed task and finds the duties irksome. It is better so. A seer has suggested that the voices of earth are dulled that we may hear the whisper of God; earth's colors are toned down that we may see things invisible.

Solitude is a wise teacher. Going apart the youth grows great. Emerson speaks of sailing the sea with God alone. The founders of astronomy dwelt on a plain of sand, where the horizon held not one vine-clad hill nor alluring vista. Wearying of the yellow sea, their thoughts journeyed along the heavenly highway and threaded the milky way, until the man became immortal. Moses became the greatest of jurists, because during the forty years when his mind was creative and at its best, he dwelt amid the solitude of the sand hills around Sinai, and was free for intellectual and moral life. History tells of a thousand men who have maintained virtue in adversity only to go down in hours of prosperity. That is, man is stimulated by the crisis; conflict provokes heroism, persecution lends strength. But, denied the exigency of a great trial, men who seemed grand fall all to pieces. Triumphant in adversity, men are vanquished by drudgery. An English author has expressed the belief that many men "achieve reputations when all eyes are focused upon them, who fall into petty worthlessness amid obscurity and monotony. Life's crowning victory belongs to those who have won no brilliant battle, suffered no crushing wrong; who have figured in no great drama, whose sphere was obscure, but who have loved great principles midst small duties, nourished sublime hopes amid vulgar cares, and illustrated eternal principles in trifles."

Responsibility is a teacher of righteousness. God educates men by casting them upon their own resources. Man learns to swim by being tossed into life's maelstrom and left to make his way ashore. No youth can learn to sail his life-craft in a lake sequestered and sheltered from all storms, where other vessels never come. Skill comes through sailing one's craft amidst rocks and bars and opposing fleets, amidst storms and whirls and counter currents. English literature has a proverb about the incapacity of rich men's sons. The rich man himself became mighty because he began in poverty, had no hand to help him forward, and many hands to hold him back. After long wrestling with opposing force he compacted within himself the strength and foresight, the frugality and wisdom of a score of ordinary men. The school of hard knocks made him a man of might. But his son, cradled in a soft nest, sheltered from every harsh wind, loving ease more than industry, is in danger of coming up without insight into the secrets of his profession or industry.

Responsibility alone drives man to toil and brings out his best gifts. For this reason the pensions given to scholars are said to have injured some men of genius. Johnson wrote his immortal Rasselas to raise money to buy his mother's coffin. Hunger and pain drove Lee to the invention of his loom. Left a widow with a family to support, in mid-life Mrs. Trollope took to authorship and wrote a score of volumes. The most piteous tragedy in English literature is that of Coleridge. Wordsworth called him the most myriad-minded man since Shakespeare, and Lamb thought him "an archangel slightly damaged." The generosity of his friends gave the poet a home and all its comforts without the necessity of toil. Is it possible that ease and lack of responsibility, with opium, helped wreck him? What did that critic mean when he said of a rich young friend, "He needs poverty alone to make him a great painter?" It is responsibility that teaches caution, foresight, prudence, courage, and turns feeblings into giants.

The extremes and contrasts of life do much to shape character. Ours is a world that moves from light to dark, from heat to cold, from summer to winter. On the crest to-day, the hero is in the trough to-morrow. Moses, yesterday a deserted slave child, to-day adopted by a king's daughter; David, but yesterday a shepherd boy with his harp, and to-day dwelling in the King's palace; men yesterday possessed of plenty, to-day passing into penury--these illustrate the extremes of life. These contrasts are as striking as those we find on the sunny slopes of the Alps. There the foothills are covered with vineyards, while the summits have everlasting snow. In Wyoming hot springs gush close beside snowdrifts. During man's few years, and brief, he experiences many reverses. He flits on between light and dark. It is hard for the leader to drop back into the ranks. It is not easy for him who hath led a movement to its success to see his laurels fall leaf by leaf. After a long and dangerous service men grown old and gray are succeeded by the youth to whom society owes no debt. Thus man journeys from strength to invalidism, from prosperity to adversity, from joy to sorrow, or goes from misery to happiness, from defeat to victory.

Not one single person but sooner or later is tested by these alterations. God sends prosperity to lift character to its highest levels. It is an error to suppose that the higher manhood flourishes in extreme poverty. Watkinson has beautifully said that "humility is never so lovely as when arrayed in scarlet; moderation is never so impressive as when it sits at banquets; simplicity is never so delightful as when it dwells amidst magnificence; purity is never so divine as when its unsullied robes are worn in a king's palace; gentleness is never so touching as when it exists in the powerful. When men combine gold and goodness, greatness and godliness, genius and graces, human nature is at its best." On the other hand, adversity is a supplement, making up what prosperity lacks. The very abundance of Christmas gifts ofttimes causes children to forget the parents who gave them. Some are adorned by prosperity as mountains are adorned with rich forests. Others stand forth with the bareness, but also with the grandeur and enduring strength, of Alpine mountains. Character is like every other structure--nothing tests it like extremes.

When friendship and love have enriched man, and deepened all the secret springs of his being, when grief hath refined and suffering mellowed him, then God sends the ideals to stimulate men to new achievements. An ideal is a pattern or plan held up before the man's eye for imitation, realization and guidance. In the heart's innermost temple of silence, whither neither friend nor enemy may ever come, there the soul unveils its secret ideal. The pattern there erected at once proclaims what man is and prophesies what he shall be. In old age men think what they are, but in youth, what we think, we come to be. Therefore must the pattern held up before the mind's eye be of the highest and purest. The legend tells us of the master's apprentice, who, from the small bits of glass that had been thrown away constructed a window of surpassing loveliness. The ideal held up before the boy's mind organized and brought together these broken bits, and wrought them into lines of perfect beauty.

Thus by his inner aspirations, man lives and builds. The inner eye reveals to the toiler a better tool or law or reform, and the realization of these visions gives social progress. The vision of conscience reveals new possibilities of character, and these give duty. The vision of the heart reveals new possibilities of friendship, and these give the home. As the sun standing upon the horizon orbs itself, first in each dewdrop, and afterward lifts the whole earth forward, so the ideal repeats itself, first in the individual heart, and afterward lifts all society forward. Thus unto man slowly building up his character comes the supreme ideal, when Jesus Christ stands forth fully revealed in His splendor. He is no empty abstraction, no bloodless theory, but bone of our bone, brother of our own body and breath, yet marred by no weakness, scarred by no sin, tossing back temptations as some Gibraltar tosses back the sea's billows and the bits of drift-wood. Strong, He subdued His strength in the day of battle, and bore Himself like iron. Yet He was so gentle that His white hand felt the fall of the rose leaf, while He inflected His gianthood to the needs of the little child. Nor could He be holden of the bands of death, for He clove a pathway through the grave, and made death's night to shine like the day. "I have but one passion," said Tholuck. "It is He! it is He!" As Shakespeare first reveals to the young poet his real riches of imagination, as Raphael first unveils to the young artist the possibilities of color, so man knows not his infinite capabilities until Jesus Christ stands forth in all His untroubled splendor. Having Him, man has not only his Teacher and Saviour, but also his Master and Model, fulfilling all the needs of the highest manhood and the noblest character.

FOOTNOTES:

[2] Modern Painters, vol. III, pg. 368.

ASPIRATIONS AND IDEALS

"As some most pure and noble face, Seen in the thronged and hurrying street, Sheds o'er the world a sudden grace, A flying odor sweet, Then passing leaves the cheated sense Balked with a phantom excellence.

'So in our soul, the visions rise Of that fair life we never led; They flash a splendor past our eyes, We start, and they are fled; They pass and leave us with blank gaze, Resigned to our ignoble days."

--The Fugitive Ideal, by Wm. Watson.

"Contentment and aspiration are in every true man's life."

"No bird can race in the great blue sky against a noble soul. The eagle's wing is slow compared with the flight of hope and love."--Swing.

"We figure to ourselves The thing we like, and then we build it up-- As chance will have it, on the rock or sand; For time is tired of wandering o'er the world, And home-bound fancy runs her bark ashore."

--Taylor.

III

ASPIRATIONS AND IDEALS.

Man is a pilgrim journeying toward the new and beautiful city of the Ideal. Aspiration, not contentment, is the law of his life. To-day's triumph dictates new struggles to-morrow. The youth flushed with success may couch down in the tent of satisfaction for one night only; when the morning comes he must fold his tent and push on toward some new achievement. That man is ready for his burial robes who lets his present laurels satisfy him. God has crowded the world with antidotes to contentment and with stimulants to progress. The world is not built for sluggards. The earth is like a road, a poor place for sleeping in, a good thing to travel over. The world is like a forge, unfit for residence, but good for putting temper in a warrior's sword. Life is built for waking up dull men, making lazy men unhappy, and the low-flying miserable. When other incitements fail, fear and remorse following behind scourge men forward; but ideals in front are the chief stimulants to growth. Each morning, waking, the soul sees the ideal man one ought to be rising in splendor to shame the man one is. Columbus was tempted forward by the floating branches, the drifting weeds, the strange birds, unto the new world rich in tropic-treasure. So by aspirations and ideals God lures men forward unto the soul's undiscovered country. In the long ago the star moving on before guided the wise men of the East to the manger where the young child lay; and still in man's night God hangs aspirations--stars for guiding men away from the slough of content to the hills of paradise. The soul hungers for something vast, and ideals lure to the long voyage, the distant harbor, and are the stars by which the pilgrim shapes his course.

Life's great teachers are friendship, occupation, travel, books, marriage, and chiefly heart-hungers. These yearnings within are the springs of all man's progress without. Sometimes philosophers say that the history of civilization is the history of great men. Confessing this, let us go on and note that the history of all great men is the history of their ideal hours, realized in conduct and character. Waking at midnight in his bleak garret, the vision splendid rose before John Milton. The boy of twelve would fain write a poem that the world would not willingly let die. He knew that whoever would write a heroic poem must first live a heroic life. From that hour the youth followed the ideal that led him on, pursuing knowledge unceasingly for seven years, never closing book before midnight, leaving Cambridge with the approbation of the good, and without stain or spot upon his life. Afterward, making a pilgrimage to Italy for study in that land of song and story, he heard of the civil wars in England, and at once returned, putting away his ambition for culture because he thought it base to be traveling in ease and safety abroad while his fellow-citizens were fighting for liberty at home. When he resisted a brutal soldier's attack who lifted his sword to say, "I have power to kill you," the scholar replied: "And I have power to be killed and to despise my murderer." Growing old and blind, and falling upon evil days and tongues, out of his heroic life he wrote his immortal poem. Dying, he still pursued his ideal, for moving into the valley and shadow, the blind poet whispered: "Still guides the heavenly vision!"

Did men but know it, this is the secret of all heroic greatness. Here is that matchless old Greek, Socrates, sitting in the prison talking with his friends of death and immortality, of the truth and beauty he hopes to find beyond. With one hand he rubs his leg, chafed by the harsh fetters, with the other he holds the cup of poison. When the sun touched the horizon he took the cup of death from the jailer's hand, and with shining face went down into the valley, and midst the thick shadows passed forever from mortal sight, still pursuing his vision splendid. And here is that pure-white martyr girl, painted by Millais, staked down in the sea midst the rising tide, but looking toward the open sky, with a great, sweet light upon her face. Here is Luther surrounded by scowling soldiers and hungry, wolfish priests, looking upward and then flinging out his challenge, "I cannot and I will not recant, God help me." Here is John Brown, with body all pierced with bullets and grievously sore, stooping to kiss the child as he went on to the gallows, with heart as high as on his wedding day. And here is that Christian nurse who followed the line of battle close up to the rifle-pits, and kindled her fire and prepared hot drinks for dying men; who, when asked by the colonel who told her to build those fires, made answer: "God Almighty, sir!" and went right on to fulfill her vision. And here is Livingstone, with his grand craggy head and deep-set eyes, found in the heart of Africa, dead beside his couch, with ink scarcely dry on words that interpreted his vision: "God bless all men who in any way help to heal this open sore of the world!" Chiefly, there is Christ, who, from the hour when the star stayed by His manger in Bethlehem, and the light ne'er seen on land or sea shone on the luminous and transfigured mount, on to the day of His uplifted cross, ever followed the divine vision that brought Him at last to Olivet, to the open sky, the ascending cloud, the welcoming heavens.

But God, who hath appointed visions unto great men, doth set each lesser human life between its dream and its task. Deep heart-hungers are quickened within the people, and then some patriot, reformer, or hero, is raised up to feed the aspiration. Afterward history stores up these noble achievements of yesterday as soul food for to day. The heart, like the body, needs nourishment, and finds it in the highest deeds and best qualities of those who have gone before. Thus the artist pupil is fed by his great master. The young soldier emulates his brave general. The patriot is inspired by his heroic chief. History records the deeds of noble men, not for decorating her pages, but for strengthening the generations that come after. The measure of a nation's civilization is the number of heroes it has had, whose qualities have been harvested for children and youth.

Full oft one hero has transformed a people. The blind bard singing through the villages of Greece met a rude and simple folk. But Homer opened up a gallery in the clouds, and there unveiled Achilles as the ideal Greek. It became the ambition of every Athenian boy to fix the Iliad in his mind and repeat Achilles in his heart and life. Soon the Achilles in the sky looked down upon 20,000 young Achilles walking through the streets beneath. With what admiration do men recall the intellectual achievements of Athens! What temples, and what statues in them! What orators and eloquence! What dramas! What lyric poems! What philosophers! Yet one ideal man who never lived, save in a poet's vision, turned rude tribes into intellectual giants. Thus each nation hungers for heroes. When it has none God sends poets to invent them as soul food for the nation's youth. The best gift to a people is not vineyards nor overflowing granaries, nor thronged harbors, nor rich fleets, but a good man and great, whose example and influence repeat greatness in all the people. As the planet hanging above our earth lifts the sea in tidal waves, so God hangs illustrious men in the sky for raining down their rich treasure upon society.

Moreover, it is the number and kind of his aspirations that determine a man's place in the scale of manhood. Lowest of all is that great under class of pulseless men, content to creep, and without thought of wings for rising. Mere drifters are they, creatures of circumstance, indifferently remaining where birth or events have started them. Having food and raiment, therewith they are content. No inspirations fire them, no ideals rebuke them, no visions of possible excellence or advancement smite their vulgar contentment. Like dead leaves swept forward upon the current, these men drift through life. Not really bad, they are but indifferently good, and therefore are the material out of which vicious men are made. In malarial regions, physicians say, men of overflowing health are safe because the abounding vitality within crowds back the poison in the outer air, while men who live on the border line between good health and ill, furnish the conditions for fevers that consume away the life. Similarly, men who live an indifferent, supine life, with no impulses upward, are exposed to evil and become a constant menace to society.

Higher in the scale of manhood are the men of intermittent aspirations. A traveler may journey forward guided by the light of the perpetual sun, or he may travel by night midst a thunder-storm, when the sole light is an occasional flash of lightning, revealing the path here and the chasm there. But once the lightning has passed the darkness is thicker than before. And to men come luminous hours, rebuking the common life. Then does the soul revolt from any evil thought and thing and long for all that is God-like in character, for honor and purity, for valor and courage, for fidelity to the finer convictions deep hidden in the soul's secret recesses. What heroes are these--in the vision hour! With what fortitude do these soldiers bear up under blows--when the battle is still in the future! But once the conflict comes, their courage goes! On a winter's morning the frost upon the window pane shapes forth trees, houses, thrones, castles, cities, but these are only frost. So before the mind the imagination hangs pictures of the glory and grandeur and God-likeness of the higher life, but one breath of temptation proves their evanescence. Better, however, these intermittent ideals than uninterrupted supineness and contentment. But, best of all, that third type of men who realize in daily life their luminous hours, and transmute their ideals into conduct and character. These are the soul-architects who build their thoughts and deeds into a plan; who travel forward, not aimlessly, but toward a destination; who sail, not anywhither, but toward a port; who steer, not by the clouds, but by the fixed stars. High in the scale of manhood these who ceaselessly aspire toward life's great Exemplar.

Consider the use of the soul's aspirations. Ideals redeem life from drudgery. Four-fifths of the human race are so overbodied and under-brained that the mind is exhausted in securing provision for hunger and raiment. No to-morrow but may bring men to sore want. Poverty narrows life into a treadmill existence. Multitudes of necessity toil in the stithy and deep mine. Multitudes must accustom themselves to odors offensive to the nostril. Men toil from morning till night midst the din of machinery from which the ear revolts. Myriads dig and delve, and scorn their toil. He who spends all his years sliding pins into a paper, finds his growth in manhood threatened. Others are stranded midway in life. Recently the test exhibition of a machine was successful, and those present gave the inventor heartiest congratulations. But one man was present whose face was drawn with pain, and whose eyes were wet with tears. Explaining his emotion to a questioner he said: "One hour ago I entered this room a skilled workman; this machine sends me out that door a common laborer. For years I have been earning five dollars a day as an expert machinist. By economy I hoped to educate my children into a higher sphere, but now my every hope is ruined." Life is crowded with these disappointments. A journey among men is like a journey through a harvest field after a hailstorm has flailed off all the buds and leaves, and pounded the young corn into the ground. Fulfilling such a life, men need to be saved by hopes and aspirations. Then God sends visions in to give men wing-room, and lift them into the realm of restfulness. Some hope rises to break the thrall of life. The soul rises like a songbird in the sky.

Disappointed men find that food itself is not so sweet as dreams. The seamstress toiling in the attic stitches hope in with each thread, and dreams of some knight coming to lift her out of poverty, and her reverie mocks and consumes her woe. The laborer digging in his ditch sweetens his toil and rests his weariness by the dream of the humble home labor and love will some day build. Many in middle life, when it is too late, find themselves in the wrong occupation, but maintain their usefulness and happiness by surrounding themselves with the thoughts of the career they love and beyond may yet fulfill. How does imagination enterprise everywhither! By it what ships are built, what lands are explored, what armies are led, what thrones are erected in thought! When the seed sprang up in the prison cell, the scholar confined there enlarged the little plant until in his mind it became a vast forest, where all flowers bloomed and spiced shrubs grew and birds sang, and where brooks gurgled such music as never fell on mortal ear. Innumerable men endure by seeing things invisible. They retire from the vexations and disappointments without to their hidden-vision life. Their inner thoughts contrast strangely with the outer fact and life. During the Middle Ages, when persecution broke out against the Jews, these merchants were oppressed and robbed, and saved themselves from destruction only by living a squalid life outside and a princely life in hidden quarters. It has been said: "You might follow an old merchant, spotted and stained with all the squalor of beggary upon him, through byways foul to the feet and offensive to every sense, and through some narrow lane enter what looks like the entrance of an ill-kept stable. Thence opens out a squalid hall of noisome odors. But ascending the steps you come to a secret passage, when, opening the door, you are blinded with the brilliancy that bursts upon you. You are in the palace of a prince. The walls are covered with adornments. Rare tapestries hang upon the walls. The dishes that bespread the table are of silver and gold, and the household, who hasten to receive the parent and strip off his outward disguise, are themselves arrayed like king's children." Thus the ideals make a great difference between the man without and the hidden life within. Seeing unseen things, the heart sings while the hand works. The vision above lifts the life out of fatigue into the realm of joy and restfulness.

It is also the office of these divine ideals to rebuke the lower physical life, and smite each sordid, selfish purpose. The vision hour is the natural enemy of the vulgar mood. Men begin life with the high purpose of living nobly, generously, openly. Full of the choicest aspirations, hungering for the highest things, the youth enters triumphantly upon the pathway of life. But journeying forward he meets conflict and strife, envy and jealousy, disappointment and defeat. He finds it hard to live up to the level of his best moods. Self-interest biases his judgment. Greed bribes reason. Pride leads him astray. Selfishness tempts him to violate his finer self. The struggle to maintain his ideals is like a struggle for life itself. Many, alas! after a short, sharp conflict, give up the warfare and break faith and fealty with the deeper convictions. They quench the light that shone afar off to beckon and cheer them on. Persuading themselves that the ideal life is impracticable, they strike an average between their highest moods and their low-flying hours. Then is the luster of life all dimmed, and the soul is like a noble mansion in the morning after some banquet or reception. In the evening, when making ready for the brilliant feast, all the house is illuminated. Each curio is in its niche. The harp is in its place. The air is laden with the perfume of roses. But when the morning comes, how vast is the change! The windows are darkened and the halls deserted; the wax tapers have burned to the socket, or flicker out in smoke; the flowers, scorched by the heated air, have shriveled and fallen, and in the banquet-room only the "broken meats" remain. Gone is all the glory of the feast! Thus, when men lay aside their heroic ideals and bury their visions, the luster of life departs, and its beauty perishes. Then it is that God sends in the heavenly vision to rebuke the poorer, sensuous life and man's material mood. Above the life that is, God hangs the glory, and grandeur, and purity of the life that might be, and the soul looking up scorns the lower things, and hungers and thirsts for truth and purity. Then man comes to himself again, and makes his way back to his Father's side.

Moreover, these vision hours come to men to give them hints and gleams of what they shall be when time and God's resources have wrought their purpose of strength and beauty upon the soul. Man is born a long way from himself and needs to see the end toward which he moves. He has a body and uses a lower life, but man is what he is in his best hours and most exalted moods. The measure of strength in any living thing is its highest faculty. The strength of the deer is swiftness, of a lion strength; but to the power of the foot the eagle adds wings, and therefore is praised for its swift flight. To the wing the bee adds genius for building with geometric skill, and its praise lies in its rare intelligence. Thus man also is to be measured by his highest faculty, in that he has power to see things unseen and work in realms invisible. We are told that Cicero had three summer villas and a winter residence, but he prided himself not upon his wealth, but upon his oratory and eloquence. The grand old statesman of England has skill for lifting the axe upon the tall trees, but he glories in his skill in statecraft. Incidentally man reaps treasures from the fields, finds riches in the forests, and wealth in the mountains; yet his real manhood resides in reason and moral sentiment, and the spirit that saith, "Our Father." For him to live for the body is as if one who should inherit a magnificent palace were to close the galleries and libraries and splendid halls, and opening only the eating-room, there to live and feed.

Happy the man who is a good mechanic or merchant; but, alas! if he is only that. Happy he who prospers toward the granary and the storehouse; but, alas! if he is shrunken and shriveled toward the spiritual realm. To all rich in physical treasure, but bankrupt toward the unseen realm, comes some divine influence arousing discontent. Then lower joys are seen to be uncrowned, and sordid pleasures to have no scepter. The soul becomes restless and disappointed where once it was contented. Looking afar off it sees in its vision hours the goodly estate to which God shall some day bring it. Here we recall the peasant's dream. His humble cottage while he slept lifted up its thatched roof and became a noble mansion. The one room and small became many and vast. The little windows became arched and beautiful, looking out upon vast estates all his. The fireplace became an altar, o'er which hung seraphim. The chimney became a golden ladder like that which Jacob saw, and his children, living and dead, passed like angels bringing treasure up and down. And thus, while the human heart muses and dreams, God builds His sanctuary in the soul. The vision the heart sees is really the pattern by which God works. These fulfill the transformation wrought in the peasant's dream.

Seeking to fulfill their noble ministry, ideals have grievous enemies. Among these let us include vanity and pride. When the wise man said, "Seest thou a man wise in his own conceit, there is more hope of a fool than of him," he indicated that he had known fools cured of their folly, but never a vain man cured of his vanity. Pliny said: "It is as hard to instruct pride as it is to fill an empty bottle with a cork in it." Some men are constitutionally vain. They think all creation converges toward one center, and they are that center. The rash of conceit commonly runs its course very early in life. With most it is like the prancing and gayety of an untrained colt; the cure is the plow and harness. Failure also is a curative agent, and so also is success. But chiefly do the ideals rebuke conceit. The imagination is God in the soul, and lifting up the possible achievement, the glory of what men may become, shames and makes contemptible what men are.

Indolence and contentment also antagonize the ideals. Men bring together a few generosities and integrities. Soul-misers, men gloat over these, as money-misers over their shining treasure, content with the little virtue they have. But no man has a right to fulfill a stagnant career; life is not to be a puddle, but a sweet and running stream. No man has a right to rust; he is bound to keep his tools bright by usage. No man has a right to be paralyzed; he is bound to enlarge and grow. So ideals come in to compel men to go forward. It is easier to lie down in a thorn hedge, or to sleep in a field of stinging nettles, than for a man to abide contentedly as he is while his ideals scourge him upward.

Chiefly do the malign elements oppose the ideal life. There is enmity between vulgarity and visions. If anger comes, mirth goes; when greed is in the ascendency, generosity is expelled. If, during a chorus of bird-voices in the forest, only the shadow of an approaching hawk falls upon the ground, every sweet voice is hushed. Thus, if but one evil, hawk-like note is heard in the heart, all the nobler joys and aspirations depart. The higher life is at enmity with the lower, and this war is one of extermination.

Oh, all ye young hearts! guard well one rock that is fatal to all excellence. If ever you have broken faith with your ideals, lift them up and renew faith. Cherish ideals as the traveler cherishes the north star, and keep the guiding light pure and bright and high above the horizon. The vessel may lose its sails and masts, but if it only keeps its course and compass, the harbor may be reached. Once it loses the star for steering by, the voyage must end in shipwreck. For when the heroic purpose goes, all life's glory departs. Let no man think the burial of a widow's son the saddest sight on earth. Let men not mourn over the laying of the first born under the turf, as though that were man's chiefest sorrow. Earth knows no tragedy like the death of the soul's ideals. Therefore, battle for them as for life itself! The cynic may ridicule them, because, having lost his own purity and truth, he naturally thinks that none are pure or true; but wise men will take counsel of aspirations and ideals. Even low things have power for incitement. No dead tree in the forest so unsightly but that some generous woodbine will wrap a robe of beauty about its nakedness. No cellar so dark but if there is a fissure through which the sunlight falls the plant will reach up its feeble tendrils to be blessed by the warming ray. Yet the soul is from God, is higher than vine or tree, and should aspire toward Him who stirs these mysterious aspirations in the heart.

The soul is like a lost child. It wanders a stranger in a strange land. Full oft it is heartsick, for even the best things content it for but a little while. Daily, mysterious ideals throb and throb within. It struggles with a vagrant restlessness. It goes yearning after what it does not find. A deep, mysterious hunger rises. It would fain come to itself. In its ideal hours it sees afar off the vision that tempts it on and up toward home and heaven. The secret of man is the secret of his vision hours. These tell him whence he came--and whither he goes. Then Christ became the soul's guide; God's heart, the soul's home.

THE PHYSICAL BASIS OF CHARACTER

"Health is the vital principle of bliss."--Thompson.

"Good nature is often a mere matter of health. With good digestion men are apt to be good natured; with bad digestion, morose."--Beecher.

"A man so trained in youth that his body is the ready servant of his will, and does with equal ease and pleasure all the work that as a mechanism it is capable of,--whose intellect is a clear, cold, logic-engine, with all its parts of equal strength and in smooth working order, ready like a steam engine to be turned to any kind of work, and spin the gossamers as well as forge the anchors of the mind."--Huxley.

"Finally, I have one advice which is of very great importance. You are to consider that health is a thing to be attended to continually, as the very highest of all temporal things. There is no kind of an achievement equal to perfect health. What to it are nuggets or millions?"--Carlyle's Address to Students at Edinburgh.

"Though I look old, yet I am strong and lusty: For in my youth I never did apply Hot and rebellious liquors in my blood: Nor did not with unbashful forehead woo The means of weakness and debility; Therefore my age is as a lusty winter, Frosty but kindly."

--"As You Like It," ii: 3.

IV

THE PHYSICAL BASIS OF CHARACTER

Ancient society looked upon the human body with the utmost veneration. The citizen of Thebes or Memphis knew no higher ambition than a competency for embalming his body. Men loved unto death and beyond it the physical house in which the soul dwelt. Every instinct of refinement and self-respect revolted from the thought of discarding the body like a cast-off garment or worn-out tool. In his dying hour it was little to Rameses that his career was to be pictured on obelisk and preserved in pyramid, but it was very much to the King that the embalmer should give permanency to the body with which his soul had gone singing, weeping and loving through three-score years and ten. The papyrus found in the tombs tells us that the soldiers of that far-off age did not fear death itself more than they feared falling in some secluded spot where the body, neglected and forgotten, would quickly give its elements back to air and earth. How noble the sentiment that attached dignity and honor to hand and foot! Sacred, doubly sacred, was the body that had served the soul long and faithfully!

The soul is a city, and as Thebes had many gateways through which passed great caravans laden with goodly treasure, so the five senses are gateways through which journey all earth's sights and sounds. Through the golden gate of the ear have gone what noble truths, companying together what messengers of affection, what sweet friendships. The eye is an Appian Way over which have gone all the processions of the seasons. How do hand and vision protect man? Hunters use sharp spears for keeping back wild beasts, but Livingstone, armed only with eye beams, drove a snarling beast into the thicket, and Luther, lifting his great eyes upon an assassin, made the murderer flee. What flute or harp is comparable for sweetness to the voice? It carries warning and alarm. It will speak for you, plead for you, pray for you. Truly it is an architect, fulfilling Dante's dictum, "piling up mountains of melody." Serving the soul well, the body becomes sacred by service. Therefore man loves and guards the physical house in which he lives.

Always objects and places associated with life's deep joys and sorrows become themselves sacred through these associations. The flock passing through the forest leaves some white threads behind. The bird lines its nest with down from its own bosom. Thus the heart, going forward, leaves behind some treasure, and perfumes its path. Memory hangs upon the tree the whispered confession made beneath its branches. No palace so memorable as the little house where you were reared, no charter oak so historic as the trees under which you played, no river Nile so notable as the little brook that once sung to your sighing, no volume or manuscript so precious as the letter and Testament your dying father pressed into your hand. Understanding this principle, nations guard the manuscript of the sage, the sword of the general, the flag stained with heroes' blood. Memorable forever the little room where Milton wrote, the cottage where Shakespeare dwelt, the spot where Dante dreamed, the ruin where Phidias wrought. But no building ever showed such comely handiwork as the temple built by divine skill. God hath made the soul's house fair to look upon. Death may close its doors, darken its windows, and pull down its pillars; still, its very ruins are precious, to be guarded with jealous care. How sacred the spot where lie the parents that tended us, the bosom that shielded our infancy, the hands that carried our weakness everywhither. Men will always deem the desecration of the body or the grave blasphemous. The physical house, standing, is the temple of God; falling, it must forever be sacred in man's memory.

Science teaches us to look upon the body as a thinking machine. As a mental mechanism it exhibits the divine being as an inventor, who has produced a machine as much superior to Watt's engine, as that engine is superior to a clod or stone. In this divine mechanism all intricate and enduring machines are combined in one. Imagine an instrument so delicate as to be at once a telescope and microscope, at one moment witnessing the flight of a sun hundreds of millions of miles away, then quickly adjusted for seeing the point of the finest needle! Imagine a machine that at one and the same moment can feel the gratefulness of the blazing fire, taste the sweetness of an orange, experience the aesthetic delights of a picture, recall the events in the careers of the men the artist has delineated, recognize the entrance of a group of friends, out of the confusion of tongues lead forth a voice not heard for years, thrill with elation at the unexpected meeting! The very mention of such an instrument, combining audiphone, telephone, phonograph, organ, loom, and many other mechanisms yet to be invented, seems like some tale from the "Arabian Nights." Yet the body and brain make up such a wondrous mental loom, weaving thought-textures called conversations, poems, orations, making the creations of a Jacquard loom mere child's play. The body is like a vast mental depot with lines running out into all the world. Everything outside has a desk inside where it transacts its special line of business. There is a visual desk where sunbeams make up their accounts; an aural desk where melodies conduct their negotiations; a memory desk where actions and motives are recorded; a logical desk where reasons and arguments are received and filed. Truly God hath woven the bones and sinews that fence the soul about into a mechanism "fearfully and wonderfully made."

To-day science is writing for us the story of the ascent of the body. Scholars perceive that matter has fulfilled its mission now that dust stands erect, throbbing in a thinking brain, and beating in a glowing heart. Ours is a world wherein God hath ordained that acorns should go on toward oaks, huts become houses, tents temples, babes men, and the generations journey on to that sublime event "toward which the whole creation moves." In this long upward march science declares the human body has had its place. Professor Drummond, famed for his Christian faith, in his recent volume tells us that man's body brings forward and combines in itself all the excellencies of the whole lower animal creation. As the locomotive of to-day contains the engine of Watt and the improvements of all succeeding inventors; as the Hoe printing-press contains the rude hand-machine of Guttenberg and the best features of all the machines that followed it; so the human body contains the special gift of all earlier and lower forms of animal life. In making a reaper the machinist does not begin with the sickle, and then unite the hook with the scythe, afterward joining thereto the rude reaper and so move on through all the improving types. But in the germinal man, nature does adopt just this method. As the embryo life develops it passes into and through the likeness of each lower animal, and ever journeying upward carries with it the special grace and gift of each creature it has left behind, "sometimes a bone, or a muscle, or a ganglion," until the excellencies of many lower forms are compacted in the one higher man. In the human body there are now seventy vestigial structures, e.g., vermiform appendices, useful in the lower life but worse than useless in man. When an anatomist discovered an organ in a certain animal he foretold its rudimentary existence in the embryonic man, and we are told his prophecy was fulfilled through the microscope, "just as the planet Neptune was discovered after its existence had been predicted from the disturbances produced in the orbit of Uranus." As some noble gallery owes its supremacy to centuries of toil and represents treasures brought in from every clime and country, so the human body represents contributions from land and sea, and members and organs from innumerable creatures that creep and walk and fly.

Thus man's descent from the animals has been displaced by the ascent of the human body. This is not degradation, but an unspeakable exaltation. Man is "fearfully and wonderfully made." God ordained the long upward march for making his body exquisitely sensitive and fitted to be the home of a divine mind. How marvelously does this view enhance the dignity of man, and clothe God with majesty and glory! It is a great thing for the inventor to construct a watch. But what if genius were given some jeweler to construct a watch carrying the power to regulate itself, and when worn out to reproduce itself in another watch of a new and higher form, endowing it at the same time with power for handing forward this capacity for self-improvement? Is not the wisdom and skill required for making a watch that is self-adjusting, self-improving, and self-succeeding vastly more than the wisdom required to construct a simple timepiece? Should science finally establish the new view, already adopted by practically all biologists, it will but substitute the method of gradualism and an unfolding progression for a human body created by an instantaneous and peremptory fiat. But this is a question for specialists and experts. Those scholars who accept this view, including such thinkers as the late President McCosh, of Princeton; Dana, of Yale; such teachers as Caird, Drummond, and scores who could be named, all renowned for their Christian belief and life, find that these new views do not waste faith, but rather nourish it. Formerly men feared and fought Newton's doctrine of gravity, trembling lest that principle should destroy belief. To-day many are troubled because of the new views of development. But it is possible for one to believe in evolution, and still believe in God with all the mind and soul and strength. Strangely enough, some are unwilling to have ascended progressively from an animal, but quite willing to have come up directly from the clod. But either origin is good enough providing man has ascended far enough from the clod and the animal, and made some approach to the angel. Some there are for whom no descent seems possible--they can go no lower; dwelling now with beasts; others seem to have made no ascent whatever, but to be even now upon the plane of things that crawl and creep. Let us leave the question to the scientists. By whatever way the body came, mentality and spirituality have now been engrafted upon it. Man is no longer animal, but spiritual; and the wondrous development of man upon this side of the grave is the pledge and promise of a long progress beyond the grave, when the divine spirit by his secret resources shall lead forth from men, emotions, dispositions, and aspirations as much beyond the present thought and life as the tree is beyond the seed and the low-lying roots.

In this new view of the human body, science not only exhibits the growth and perfection of man as the goal toward which God has been moving from the first, but also throws light upon the sinfulness of man and the conflicts that rage within the soul. Man is seen to be a double creature. The spirit man rides a man of flesh and is often thrown thereby and trampled under foot. There is a lower animal nature having all the appetites and passions that sustain the physical organization; but super-imposed thereon, is a spiritual man, with reason and moral sentiment, with affection and faith. The union of the two means strife and conflict; the doing what one would not do and the leaving undone what one would do. The poet describes the condition by saying: "The devil squatted early on human territory, and God sent an angel to dispossess him." The animal nature foams out all manner of passions and lusts. From thence issue also lurid lights and murky streams. But the under man is not the true man. The soldier rides the horse, but is himself other than his beast. Man uses an animal at the bottom, but man is what he is at the top. Sin is the struggle for supremacy between the animal forces and the higher spiritual powers. The passions downstairs must be subordinated to the people upstairs. In some men the animal impulses predominate with terrible force, and their control is not easy. It is as if a child should try to drive a chariot drawn by forty steeds of the sun. When a man finds that he can not dam back the mountain stream, nor stop up its springs, he learns to use the stream by building a mill, and controlling the pressure of the flood for grinding his corn. Similarly, the problem of life is for the upper man to educate, control, and transmute the lower forces into sympathy and service. The combative powers once turned against his fellows must be turned against nature and used for hewing down the forests, bridging rivers, piercing mountains. Thus every animal force and passion becomes sacred through consecration to mental and spiritual ends and aims.

Sin therefore ceases to be philosophy or medievalism; it becomes a concrete personal fact. Daily each one comes under its rule and sway. The mind loves truth, and the body tempts man to break truth. The soul loves honor, and passion tempts it to deflect its pathway. Man goes forth in the morning with all the springs of generosity open; but before night selfishness has dammed up the hidden springs. In the morning man goes out with love irradiating his face; he comes back at night sullen and black with hatred and enmity. In the morning the soul is like a young soldier, parading in stainless white; at night his garments are begrimed and soiled with self-indulgence and sin. As there is a line along the tropics where two zones meet and breed perpetual storm, so there is a middle line in man where the animal man meets the spiritual man, and there is perpetual storm. There clouds never pass away, and the thunder never dies out of the horizon of time.[3] This view, appealing to universal reason, appeals also to divine help. In his daily strife man needs the brooding presence and constant stimulus of the divine being. Man waits for God's stimulus as the frozen roots wait the drawing near of God's sun. The soul looks ever unto the hills whence cometh its help. In the morning, at noon, and at night, man longs for a deliverer. God is the pledge of the soul's victory over the body. For men floundering in the slough of sin and despond these words, "Ye may, ye must be born again," are sweeter than angel songs falling from the hills of Paradise.

Consider the uses of the body. It is God's schoolmaster teaching industry, compelling economy and thrift, and promoting all the basal moralities. It contains the springs of all material civilization. If we go back to the dawn of history we find that hunger and the desires, associated with the body, have been the chief stimulants toward industrial progress. Indolence is stagnation. Savages in the tropics are torpid and without progress. Hunger compels men to ask what food is in the river, what roots are in the ground, what fruits are on the trees, what forces are in the air. The body is peremptory in its demands. Hunger carries a stinging scourge. Necessity drives out the evil spirits of indolence and torpidity. The early man threading the thickets in search of food chanced upon a sweet plum, and because the bush grew a long way from his lodge he transplanted the root to a vale near his home. Thence came all man's orchards and vineyards. Shivering with cold, man sought out some sheltered cave or hollow tree. But soon the body asked him to hew out a second cave in addition to the one nature had provided. Fulfilling its requests, man went on in the interests of his body to pile stone on stone, and lift up carved pillars and groined arches. Thence came all homes. For the body the sower goes forth to sow, and the harvester looks forward to the time of sheaves and shoutings. For strengthening the body the shepherd leads forth his flocks and herds, and for its raiment the weaver makes the looms and spindles fly. For the body all the trains go speeding in and out, bringing fruits from the sunny south, and furs from the frozen north. All the lower virtues and integrities spring from its desires. As an engine, lying loose in a great ship, would have no value, but, fastened down with bolts, drives the great hull through the water, so the body fastens and bolts the spirit to field, forest, and city, and makes it useful and productive. Material life and civilization may be said to literally rest upon man's bones and sinews.

The body is also the channel of all the knowledges. How scant is the child's understanding of the world-house in which he lives! There are shelves enough, but they are all empty. In the interest of intelligence his mind is sheathed in this sensitive body and the world forces without report themselves to this sensitive nerve mechanism. Fire comes in to burn man's fingers and teach him how to make the fire smite vapor from water. Cold comes in to nip his ears and pinch his cheeks until he learns the economy of ice, snow and rain. Steel cuts his fingers and the blood oozes out. Thenceforth he turns the axe toward the trees and the scythe toward the standing grain. The stone falling bruises him, compelling a knowledge of gravity and the use of trip-hammer, weights and pulleys. Looking downward the eye discerns the handwriting on the rocks and the mind reads earth's romantic story. Looking upward, the vision runs along the milky way for measuring the starry masses and searching out their movements. The ear strains out sweet sounds, and St. Cecilia hears melodies from the sky. Bending over the cradle, the parent marvels at God's bounty in the face of a babe. When the little one goes away the parent copies its face in rude colors, or carves its form in marble. Thus all the arts, sciences and inventions are gifts of the body to man's mental and moral life.

There is a beautiful story of a company of celestial beings, who, in disguise, entered an ancient city upon a mission of mercy. Departing hurriedly, in some way a fair young child was left behind and lost. In the morning when men came upon the streets they found a sweet boy with sunny hair sitting upon the steps of the temple. Language had he none. He answered questions with streaming eyes and frightened face. While men wondered a slave drew near, carrying a harp. Then the heavenly child signaled for the instrument, for this language he could speak. He threw his arms about the harp as the child about its mother's neck. He touched one string. Upon the hushed air there stole out a note pure, clear, and sweet as though amethysts and pearls were melted into liquid melodies. It was music, but not such music as mortals give to mortals. It was such a song as spirit would sing to spirit, signaling across the streets of heaven. It was a hymn to the mother whom he had loved and lost. With tearful eye and smiling face the little stranger and the harp together wept, and laughed, and sobbed out their grief and song. It was the speech of a child homesick for heaven. What that harp was to the silent boy, the human body is to man's soul within. The soul teemed with thoughts. Fancies surged and thronged within. Then God gave the soul a body, as a harp of many strings. Through it the soul finds voice and pours forth its rich thoughts and varied emotions.

Consider, also, how nature has ordained the body as a system of moral registration. Nature has a record of all men's deeds, keeping her accounts on fleshly tablets. The mind may forget, the body never. The brain sees to it that the thoughts within do immediately dispose of facial tissue without. Mental brightness gives facial illumination. The right act or true thought sets its stamp of beauty in the features; the wrong act or foul thought sets its seal of distortion. Moral purity and sweetness refine and beautify the countenance. The body is a show window, advertising and exhibiting the soul's stock of goods. Nature condenses bough, bud and shrub into black coal; compacts the rich forces of air and sun and soil into peach and pear. In the kingdom of morals, there are people who seem to be of virtue, truth and goodness all compact. Contrariwise, every day you will meet men upon our streets who are solid bestiality and villainy done up in flesh and skin. Each feature is as eloquent of rascality as an ape's of idiocy. Experts skilled in physiognomy need no confession from impish lips, but read the life-history from page to page written on features "dimmed by sensuality, convulsed by passion, branded by remorse; the body consumed with sloth and dishonored with selfish uses; the bones full of the sins of youth, the face hideous with secret vices, the roots dried up beneath and the branches cut off above." It is as natural and necessary for hidden thoughts and deeds to reveal themselves through cuticle as for root or bud in spring to unroll themselves into sight and observation. Here and now everything tends to obscure nature's handwriting and to veil it in mist and disguise. But the body is God's canvas, and nature's handwriting goes ever on. Each faculty is a brush, and with it reason thinks out the portrait. Even the wolf may give something to the features, and also the snake and scorpion. Soon will come an hour when men will hear not the voice of the sirens singing praises in the ear, nor the plaudits of men of low deeds and conscience, but an hour when men shall stand in the presence of the all-revealing light and see themselves as they are and review the life they have embodied and emportraited. Happy, thrice happy, those who have traversed all life's pathway and come at last to the hour when they stand face to face with themselves, then to find therein a divine image like unto the comeliness and completion of Him whose face was transfigured and shone as the light.

At length has dawned the day when science strengthens the argument for immortality. The dream of the prophet and seer is confirmed in the light of modern knowledge. "Each new discovery," says John Fiske, "but places man upon a higher pinnacle than ever, and lights the future with the radiant color of hope." Leaving his body behind, man journeys on toward an immortal destiny. Science has emptied a thousand new meanings into the words of Socrates: "The destruction of the harp does not argue the death of the harpist." Nature decrees that the flower must fall when the fruit swells. If the winged creature is to come forth and increase, the chrysalis must perish and decrease. When the long journey is over it is natural that the box in which the richly carved and precious statue is packed should be tossed aside. Swiftly youth goes on toward maturity, age toward old age, and the scythe awaits all. But sickness and trouble can do nothing more than dim the eye, dull the ear, weaken the hand. Dying and death avail not for injuring reason, affection, or hope, or love.

At the close of a long and arduous career the famous Lyman Beecher passed under a mental cloud. The great man became as a little child. One day after his son, Henry Ward, had preached a striking sermon, his father entered the pulpit and beginning to speak wandered in his words. With great tenderness the preacher laid his hand upon his father's shoulder and said to the audience: "My father is like a man who, having long dwelt in an old house, has made preparations for entering a new and larger home. Anticipating a speedy removal, he sent on beforehand much of his soul-furniture. When later the day of removal was postponed the interval seemed so brief as to render it unnecessary to bring back his mental goods." Oh, beautiful words describing those whose strength is declining, whose spirit is ebbing and senses failing, because God is packing up their soul-furniture that they may be ready for the long journey that awaits us all. But man's journey is not unto the grave. Dying is transmutation. Dying is not folding of the wings; but pluming the pinions for new and larger flight. Dying is not striking an unseen rock, but a speedy entrance into an open harbor. Death is no enemy, letting the arrow fly toward one who sits at life's banquet-table. Death is a friend coming on an errand of release and divine convoy. For God's children "to be death-called is to be God-called; to be God-called is to be Christ-found; to be Christ-found is hope and home and heaven."

FOOTNOTES:

[3] See Symposium on Evolution, Homiletic Review, May, 1894.

THE MIND: AND THE DUTY OF RIGHT THINKING

"All ye who possess the power of thought, prize it well! Remember that its flight is infinite; it winds about over so many mountain tops, and so runs from poetry to eloquence, it so flies from star to star, it so dreams, so loves, so aspires, so hangs both over mystery and fact, that we may well call it the effort of man to explore the home, the infinite palace of his heavenly Father."--Swing.

"Men with empires in their brains."--Lowell.

"'Tis the mind that makes the body rich."--Taming of the Shrew.

"Like thoughts whose very sweetness yieldeth proof That they were born for immortality."--Wordsworth.

"Neither years nor books have yet availed to extirpate a prejudice then rooted in me that a scholar is the favorite of heaven and earth, the excellency of his country, the happiest of men."--Emerson.

"Happy is the man that findeth wisdom, for the merchandise of it is better than the merchandise of silver, and the gain thereof than fine gold."--Solomon.

V

THE MIND; AND THE DUTY OF RIGHT THINKING

With fine imagery the seer of old likened the mind unto a tree. The tree shakes down its fruits, and the mind sheds forth its thoughts. The boughs of the one will cover the land with forests; the faculties of the other will sow the world with harvests that blight or harvests that bless. The measure of personal worth, therefore, is the number and quality of thoughts issuing from man's mind. For all the doing called commerce, and all the speaking called conversation and books, begin with the thinking called ideas. Each thing was first a thought. A loom is Arkwright's thought dressed up in iron clothes. Books are the scholar's thoughts caught and fastened upon the white page. As our planet and the harvests that cover it are the thoughts of God rushing into visible expression, so all houses and ships, all cities and institutions, are man's inner thoughts, taking on outer and material embodiment.

When thoughts compacted into habits have determined character and destiny for the individual, they go on and secure their social progress. When God would order a great upward movement for society, He drops a great idea into the mind of some leader. Such energies divine have these thoughts that they create new epochs in history. Through Luther the thought of liberty in church and state set tyrants trembling and thrones tottering. Through Cromwell the thought of personal rights became a weapon powerful enough utterly to destroy that citadel of iniquity named the divine right of kings. It was a great moral thought called the "Golden Rule" that shotted the cannon of the North for victory and spiked the cannon of the South for defeat. Measureless is the might of a moral idea. It exceeds the force of earthquakes and the might of tidal waves. The reason why no scholar or historian can forecast the events and institutions of the next century is that none can tell what great idea God will drop into the soul of some man ordained to be its voice and prophet.

Now the omnipotence of thoughts is not without reason. Man is the child of genius because he is the child of God. Those beautiful words, "made in His image," tell us that the human mechanism is patterned after the divine. Reason and memory in man answer to those faculties in God, as do conscience and the moral sentiments. In creative genius man alone is a sharer with God. As the Infinite One passing through space leaves behind those shining footsteps called suns and stars, glowing and sparkling upon planets innumerable, so man's mind, moving through life, leaves behind a pathway all shining with books, laws, liberties and homes. Of all the wonderful things God hath made, man the wonderer is himself the most wonderful. No casket owned by a king, filled with gems and sparkling jewels, ever held such treasure as God hath put into this casket of bones and sinew. The imagination cannot paint in colors too rich this being, who is a miniature edition of infinity. It is not fiction, but fact, to say that reason is a loom; only where Jacquard's mechanism weaves a few yards of silk and satin, reason weaves conversation, sympathy, songs, poems, eloquence--textures all immortal. And memory is a gallery; only where the Louvre holds a few pictures of the past, memory waving her wonder-working wand brings back all faces, living and dead, causing mountains and battle-fields, with all distant scenes, to pass before the mind in solemn procession.

The Bank of England has indeed a mechanism that tests coins and throws out all light weights. But judgment is an instrument testing things invisible, weighing arguments and motives, testing principles and characters. And the desires, are they not like unto the richly laden argosies of commerce? And fancy, hath it not the skill of artist and architect? Imagination, working in the realm of the useful, turns iron into engines. Imagination, working in realms of the beautiful, turns pigments into pictures. Imagination, working in the realms of thought, can turn things true into sciences, and things good into ethical systems. Well did the philosopher say that the greatest star is the one standing at the little end of the telescope, the one looking, not looked at nor looked for. When some Agassiz dredging the Atlantic tells us what animals lived there a million years ago, the scientist's mind seems an abyss deeper than the sea itself; and when Tyndall, climbing to the top of the Matterhorn, reads on that rock-page all the events of the ancient world, the mountain is dwarfed to an ant hill and becomes insignificant in the presence of the mountain-minded scholar. Hunters tell us that when crossing a swamp they leap from one hummock of grass to another. But Herschel and Proctor, exploring the heavenly world, step from star to star. The husbandman, squeezing a cluster of grapes in his cup, does but interpret to us the way in which the scholar squeezes planets and suns to brim the cup of knowledge for man's thirsting soul. This vast and wondrous world without is matched by man's rich and various mind within! Well did Emerson exclaim, "Man, thou palace of sight and sound, carrying in thy senses the nights and mornings, the summers and winters; carrying in thy brain the geometry of the City of God, in thy heart all the bowers of love, and all the realms of right and wrong."

Such being the nature of the mind, consider its prodigious fruitfulness in thought. If all the processes of the mind were reduced to material volume, the thoughts of each moment would fill a page, the thoughts of each hour would fill a chapter, the thoughts of each day would fill a volume, the emotions of a year would fill a small library of many volumes. Value might be wanting, but not bulk. It is given to the eye to behold the harvests wrought by the secret force of roots and sunbeams. But if all the products of the soul could be made visible to the eye and ear, how marvelous would be these exhalations, rising and filling all the air. Were all the emotions and passions and dreams of one single day fully revealed, what dramas would there be beyond all the tragedies man's hand hath ever indicated! Consider what fertility the mind hath! Consider how many trains of thought reason takes up each hour. Consider all that belongs to a man as an animal, his fears and passions, defensory in nature. Consider his social equipment, with all the possible moods and combinations of affections. Consider the vast activities of his reason working outward, and the imagination working upward. Sometimes in the morning man's thoughts are for number and strength like unto the strength of armies. Sometimes in the night his aspirations exhale heavenward with all the purity and beauty of the clouds. Consider also how life's conflicts and warfare inflame man's faculties and hasten their process.

Consider how courage, despondency, hope and fear, friendship and enmity, increase the activities. Consider man's ambitions--steeds of the sun with incredible swiftness dragging forward the soul's chariot. Consider the rivalries among men. What intensities of thought are induced thereby! Consider that toward one's friends the mind sends forth thoughts that are almoners of bounty and angels of mercy. But consider that man is over against his enemy, with a mind like unto a walled city filled with armed men. Consider how in life's conflicts, thoughts become the swords of anger, the clubs of envy, stings for hissing hatred. Consider that in times of great excitement the soul literally blazes and burns, exhaling emotions and thoughts as a planet exhales light and heat. Wondrous the power of the loom newly invented, that with marvelous swiftness weaves in silk figures of flowers and trees and birds. But the uttermost speed of those flying shuttles is slowness itself compared to the swiftness of the mental loom, that without noise or clangor weaves fabrics eternal out of the warp and woof of affection and thought, of passion and purpose. Consider that every man is not simply two men, but a score of men. All the climatic disturbances in nature, all distemperatures through heat and cold, wet and dry, summer and winter, do but answer in number and variety to the moods in man's brain. Not the all-producing summer is so rich in bounty as the mind is rich in thought when working its regnant and creative moods. Vast are the buildings man's hands have reared; sweet are the songs man's mind hath sung; lovely the faces man's hand hath painted; but the silent songs the soul hears, the invisible pictures the mind sees, the secret buildings the imagination rears, these are a thousand-fold more beautiful than any as yet embodied in this material world.

The Spanish have a proverb that "He who sows thoughts will reap acts, habits, and character," for destiny itself is determined by thinking. Life is won or lost by its master thoughts. As nothing reveals character like the company we like and keep, so nothing foretells futurity like the thoughts over which we brood. It was said of John Keats that his face was the face of one who had seen a vision. So long had his inner eye been fixed upon beauty, so long had he loved that vision splendid, so long had he lived with it, that not only did his soul take on the loveliness of what he contemplated, but the very lines of the poet's face were chiseled into beauty by those sculptors called thoughts and ideals. When Wordsworth speaks of the girl's beauty as "born of murmuring sound," the poet indicates his belief that the girl's long love of the sweet briar and the thrush's song, her tender care of her favorite flowers, had ended in the saturation of her own face with sweetness. Swiftly do we become like the thoughts we love. Scholars have noticed that old persons who have "lived long together, 'midst sunshine and 'midst cloudy weather," come at length to look as nearly alike as do brother and sister: Emerson explains this likeness by saying that long thinking the same thoughts and loving the same objects mould similarity into the features. Nor is there any beauty in the face of youth or maiden that can long survive sourness in the disposition or discontent in the heart.

Contrariwise, all have seen faces very plain naturally that have become positively radiant because the beautiful soul that is enmeshed in and stands behind the muscles has shone through and beautified all of the facial tissues. Two of our great novelists have made a special study of the architectural power of thoughts. Dickens exhibits Monks as beginning his career as an innocent and beautiful child; but as ending his life as a mass of solid bestiality, a mere chunk of fleshed iniquity. It was thinking upon vice and vulgarity that transformed the angel's face into the countenance of a demon. Hawthorne has made a similar study of Chillingworth, whose moral deterioration began through evil thinking when face and physique were fully matured. Chillingworth stood forth in middle life a thoughtful, earnest, and just man; but, during his absence, he suffered a grievous wrong. Not knowing the identity of his enemy, the physician came to suspect his friend. By skillful questions he digged into Dimmesdale's heart as the sexton might delve into the grave in search of a possible jewel upon a dead man's breast. When suspicion had strengthened into certainty, enmity became hatred. Then, for two years, Chillingworth tortured his victim as once inquisitors tortured men by tweaking the flesh with red-hot pincers. Soon the face of the physician, once so gentle and just, took on an aspect sinister and malign. Children feared him, men shivered in his presence--they knew not why. Once the magistrate saw the light glimmering in his eyes "with flames that burned blue, like the ghastly fire that darted out of Bunyan's awful doorway on the hillside and quivered in the Pilgrim's face." All this is Hawthorne's way of telling us how thoughts determine character and shape destiny. He who thinks of mean and ugly things will soon show mud in the bottom of his eye. Ugliness within soon fouls the facial tissues. But he who thinks of "things true and just and lovely" will, by his thinking, be transformed into the image of the ideal he contemplates, even as the rose becomes red by exposing its bosom to the sunbeams and soaking each petal in the sun's fine rays.

Not only are thoughts the builders of character for the individual; they are also the architects of states and nations. All this wonderful fabric lying over our land like a beautiful garment is a fabric spun and woven out of ideas. Each outer substance was builded by an inner sentiment. What the eye sees are stone and brick and iron united by masons and carpenters, but the forces that hold these material things together are not iron bands, but thoughts and beliefs. Destroy the life-nerve running up through the tree, and the rings of wood will soon fall apart. Destroy the thoughts and beliefs of our people, and its homes, colleges and institutions will decline and decay. Thrust a million Mohammedans into our land, and their inner thoughts will realize themselves in mosques, minarets, and harems. But thrust a million Americans into Asia Minor and straightway their thoughts will take on these visible shapes called houses and factories, temples of learning, altars of praise and prayer. For what we call Saxon civilization is only a magnificent incarnation of a certain mental type and a moral character. Not only individuals, but nations are such stuff as thoughts are made of.

In his famous story of archery Virgil represents Acestes as shooting his arrow with such force that it took fire as it flew and went up into the air all aflame, thus opening from the place where the archer stood a pathway of light into the heavens. Now it is given to man's thoughts to fulfill this beautiful story, in that they open up shining pathways along which the human steps may move. On the practical side, it is by the thinking alone that man solves his bread-winning problem. Standing, each in his place, using his strongest faculty and working in the line of least resistance, each must conquer for himself food and support. To say that society owes us a living or to consume more than we produce is to sink to the level of pauper and parasite. The successful man is one whose thoughts about his bread-winning problem have been wise thoughts; paupers and tramps, with their hunger and rags, are men who have thought foolishly about how they could best earn a livelihood.

He who has one strong faculty, the using of which would give delight and success, yet passes it by, to use a weaker faculty, is doomed to mediocrity and heart-breaking failure. The eagle has powerful muscles under the wings, but slender and feeble legs; the fawn lacks the weight of the draught horse, but has limbs for swiftness. Now, if an eagle should become a competitor in a walking race and if the fawn should enter the list of draught horses, we should have that which answers precisely to the way in which some men seek to gain their livelihood, by tying up their strongest gift and using their feeblest faculties. When it is said that only five merchants out of a hundred succeed we perceive that the great majority of men do not think to any purpose in choosing an occupation. Recalling his friends who had misfitted themselves, Sidney Smith once said: "If we represent the occupations of life by holes in a table, some round, some square, some oblong, and persons by bits of wood of like shapes, we shall generally find that the triangular person has got into the square hole, the oblong into the triangular, while the square person has squeezed himself into the round hole." For lack of wise thinking beforehand, multitudes have died of broken hearts midst failure and misery who might have achieved great happiness and success had they used their thoughts in choosing their life-work. He who approaches his task with a leaden heart is out of the race before he is in it. Success means that the heart loves what the hand does. The bread-winning problem is the one that touches us first and most closely, and to wise thoughts only is it given to solve that problem.

The number and value of our thoughts determine a man's value to society. No investments bring so high a rate of interest as investments of brain. Hand work earns little, but head work much. In a Western camp one miner put his lower brain into the pickaxe and earned $2.00 a day; another miner put his higher brain into the stamp-mill and soon was receiving a score of dollars daily for his work; a third youth, toiling in the same mine, put his genius into an electric process for extracting ore, and sold his invention for a fortune. It seems that wealth was not in the pick, but in the thoughts that handled it. Had God intended man to do his work through the body, man's legs would have been long enough to cover leagues at a stride, his biceps would have been strong enough to turn the crank for steamships, his back would have been Atlantean for carrying freight cars across the plains.

But, instead of giving man long legs, God gave him a mind able to make locomotives. Instead of telescopic eyes, he gave man mind to invent far-seeing glasses. Instead of a thousand fingers for weaving, he gave man five fingers and genius for inventing a thousand steel fingers to do his spinning. Wealth is not in things, but in the brain that shapes raw material. Vast was the sum of gold taken out of California, but this nation might well pay down a hundred Californias for a man to invent a process to make coal drive the engine without the intervention of steam. That inventor would enable the street cars for one cent to carry the people of the tenement-house district ten miles into the country in ten minutes, and thereby, through sunshine and fresh air and solitude, would solve a hundred problems that now vex the statesman and the moralist. A young botanist in Kansas has just announced his purpose to cross the milkweed and the strawberry, so that hereafter strawberries and cream may grow upon the same bush. His task may be doomed to failure, but that youth at least understands that thought turned the wild rice into wheat; thought turned the sweet briar into the crimson rose; brains mixed the pigments for Paul Veronese, and gave the canvas worth a few florins the value of tens of thousand of dollars. Already wise thoughts have turned the barbarian into a gentleman and citizen, and some glad day thoughts will crown man with the attributes and qualities of God.

Of old, the Greek philosopher described the origin of man. One day Ceres, in crossing a stream, saw a human face emerging from the soil. It was the face of a man. Standing by this earth-born creature, the goddess extricated his head and chest; but left his legs fastened in the soil. Now, the invisible friends that free man from his earth fetters are those divine visitors called ideas and thoughts. God hath made thoughts to be golden chariots, in which the soul is swept upward into the heavenly heights.

When thoughts have sown man's pathway with happiness and peace they go on to determine character and futurity. Each life memorable for goodness and nobility has for its motive power some noble thought. Each hero has climbed up to immortality upon those golden rounds called good thoughts. Here is that cathedral spirit, John Milton. In his loneliness and blindness his mind was his kingdom. He loved to think of things true and pure and of good report. Oft at midnight upon the poet's ear there fell the sound of celestial music, that afterward he transposed into his "Paradise Regained." Dying, it was given him to proudly say: "I am not one of those who have disgraced beauty of sentiment by deformity of conduct, nor the maxims of the freeman by the actions of the slave, but by the grace of God, I have kept my soul unsullied." Here is the immortal Bunyan, spending his best years in Bedford jail because he insisted on giving men the message God had first given him; but he, too, opened his mind only to good thoughts. For him, also, dawned the heavenly vision. As the prison doors opened before Peter and the angel, so the dungeon walls parted before his thoughts. Walking about in glad freedom, he crossed the portals of the Palace Beautiful. From its marble steps he saw afar off the Delectable Mountains. Hard by ran the River of the Water of Life. The breezes of the hills of Paradise cooled his hot temples and lifted his hair. His regal thoughts crowned the Bedford tinker and made him king in English literature.

Here also is the carpenter's Son rising before each earthly pilgrim like a star in the night. A man of truly colossal intellect, incomparable as He strides across the realms and ages, yet always thinking the gentlest, kindliest thoughts; thoughts of mildness as well as of majesty; thoughts of humanity as well as divinity. His thoughts were medicines for hurt hearts; His thoughts were wings to all the low-flying; His thoughts freed those who had been snared in the thickets; His thoughts set an angel down beside each cradle; His thoughts of the incarnation rendered the human body forever sacred; His thoughts of the grave sanctified the tomb. Dying and rising, His thoughts clove an open pathway through the sky. Taught by Him, the people have learned to think--not only great thoughts, but good ones, and also how to turn thoughts into life.

Bringing their thoughts to God, God has turned thinking into character. Each spinner who in modesty and fidelity tends his loom, spins indeed, garments for others, but also weaves himself invisible garments of everlasting life. Each shipbuilder fastening his timbers together with honest thoughts will find that his thoughts have become ships carrying him over the sea to the harbor of God. Each worker putting integrity into gold and silver will find that he has carved his own character into a beauty beyond that of gems and sapphires. For his thoughts drag into futurity after them. So deeply was St. George Mivart impressed by this that he said: "The old pauper woman whom I saw to-day in the poorhouse, in her hunger saving her apple to give to the little orphan just brought in, and unraveling her stocking and bending her twisted old fingers to knit its yarn into socks for the blue feet of the child will, I verily believe, begin her life at death with more intellectual genius--mark the words, intellectual genius--than will begin that second life any statesman or prime minister or man famed in our day. For I know of none who hath been faithful in his much after the fashion of the pauper woman's fidelity with her little."

For intellect weighs light as punk against the gold of character. Should God give us to choose between goodness and genius, we may well say, "Give genius to Lucifer, let mine be the better part." Intellect is cold as the ice-palace in Quebec. Heart-broken and weary-worn by life's battle, men draw near to some great-hearted men, as pilgrims crowd close to the winter's fire. Men neither draw their chairs close around a block of ice, nor about a brilliant intellect. Our quarrel with the foolish scientist is that he makes God out as infinite brain. We rejoice at the revelation of Christ, because He portrays God as heart and not genius.

God be thanked for great thoughts, but a thousand times more, God be praised for good thoughts! They are fuel for the fires of enthusiasm. They are rudders that guide us heavenward. They are seeds for great harvests of joy. They fulfill the tale of the fairies who in the night while men slept bridged chasms, builded palaces, laid out streets and lined them with homes, built the city around with walls. For every thought is a builder, every purpose a mansion, and every affection a carpenter. As the builders of the Cologne

Cathedral were guided by the plan and pattern of Von Rile, so man's thoughts are builded after that matchless model, Jesus Christ. And while our thoughts work, His thoughts work, also adding beauty to the soul's strength. In the olden tale the artist pupil through very weariness fell asleep before the picture that disappointed him. While he slept his master stole into the room, and with a few swift touches corrected the errors and brought out the lines of lustrous beauty, kindling new hope within the boy's heart. And there are unexpected providences in life, strange influences, interventions and voices in the night. These events over which we have no control, these thoughts of the Master above, shape us not less than the thoughts that build from within. It seems that not one, but two are working upon the soul's structure. As one day in the presence of his master Michael Angelo pulled down the scaffolding in the Sistine Chapel, and the workmen cleared away the ropes and plaster and litter, and looking up men saw the faces of angels and seraphs, with their lustrous and immortal beauty, so some glad day will that angel named Death pull down life's scaffolding and set forever in the sunlight that structure built of thoughts, the stately mansion reared in the mind, the building not made with hands, the character, eternal in the heavens.

THE MORAL USES OF MEMORY

"Without memory, man is a perpetual infant."--Locke.

"The memory plays a great part in ranking men. Quintilian reckoned it the measure of genius. The poets represented the muses as the daughters of memory."--Emerson.

"Recollection is the only paradise from which we cannot be turned out."--Richter.

"A land of promise, a land of memory, A land of promise flowing with the milk And honey of delicious memories." --Tennyson.

"I have a room wherein no one enters save I myself alone; There sits a blessed memory on a throne. There my life centers." --C.G. Rosetti.

VI

THE MORAL USES OF MEMORY

The soul is a monarch whose rule includes three realms. Its throne is in the present, but its scepter extends backward over yesterday and forward over to-morrow. The divinity that presides over the past is memory; to-day is ruled by reason, to-morrow is under the regency of hope. In every age memory has been an unpopular goddess. The poet Byron pictures this divinity as sitting sorrowing midst mouldering ruins and withering leaves. But the orators unveil the future as a tropic realm, magical, mysterious and surpassingly rich. The temple where hope is worshiped is always crowded; her shrines are never without gifts of flowers and sweet songs.

But at length has come a day when man perceives that the vast treasure to which the present has fallen heir was bequeathed by that friend called yesterday. The soul increases in knowledge and culture, because as it passes through life's rich fields memory plucks the ripe treasure on either hand, leaving behind no golden sheaf. Philosophy, therefore, opposes that form of poetry that portrays yesterday by the falling tower, the yellow leaf, the setting sun. Memory is a gallery holding pictures of the past. Memory is a library holding wisdom for to-morrow's emergencies. Memory is a banqueting-hall on whose walls are the shields of vanquished enemies. Memory is a granary holding bread for to-morrow's hunger, seed for to-morrow's sowing. That man alone has a great to-morrow who has back of him a multitude of great yesterdays.

Aristotle used memory as a measure of genius. He believed that every great man was possessed of a great memory in his own department. He was the great artist whose mind searched out and whose memory retained the beauty of each sweet child, the loveliness of each maiden and mother. He was the great scientist who remembered all the facts, forgot no exception, and grouped all under laws. The great orator was he whose memory stood ready to furnish all truths gleaned from books and conversation, from travel and experience--weapons these with which the orator faces his hearers in a noble cause, controls and conquers them.

After driving through Windsor Park, Dor? the artist, recognized his debt to memory by observing that he could recall every tree he had passed, and draw each shrub from memory. We are indebted to the mechanical genius of Watt for the steam engine; but, before beginning his work, the inventive faculty asked memory to bring forward all objects, forces and facts suggested by and relating to that steaming tea kettle. Genius cannot create without material upon which to work. It is given to the eye and the ear and the reason to obtain the facts; memory stores these treasures away until they are needed; and, selecting therefrom, the inventive faculty fashions physical things into tools, beautiful things into pictures, ideas into intellectual philosophies, morals into ethical systems. The architect is helpless unless he remembers where are the quarries and what their kinds; where the marbles and what their colors; where the forests and what their trees.

Thus all the creative minds, from Phidias to Shakespeare, have united strength of memory with fertility of invention. As the Gobelin tapestry, depicting the siege of Troy, is woven out of myriads of tinted threads, so each Hamlet and each "In Memoriam" is an intellectual texture woven out of ideas and aspirations furnished by memory. Indeed, without this faculty there could be no knowledge or culture. Destroy memory and man would remain a perpetual infant. Because the mind carries forward each new idea and experience, there comes a day when the youth stands forth a master in his chosen craft or profession. It is memory that unifies man's life and thought, and binds all his experiences into one bundle.

In a large sense civilization itself is a kind of racial memory. Moving backward toward the dawn of history, we come to a time when man stood forth as a savage, his house a cave, his clothes a leather girdle, his food locusts and berries. But to-day he is surrounded by home, and books and pictures, by looms and trains and ships. Now yesterday was the friend that gave man all this rich treasure. We pluck clusters from vines other generations planted. We ride in trains and ships other thinkers invented. We admire pictures and statues other hands painted and carved. Our happiness is through laws and institutions for which other multitudes died. We sing songs that the past did write, and speak a language that generations long dead did fashion.

When De Tocqueville visited our country, he journeyed westward until he stood upon the very frontier of civilization. Before him lay the forests and prairies, stretching for thousands of miles toward the setting sun. But what impressed him most deeply was the civilization behind him, reaching to the

Atlantic--a civilization including towns and villages, with free institutions, with schoolroom and church and library. With joy he reflected that the mental and moral harvests behind him were sufficient to sow the vast unconquered land with treasure. Thus each to-day is a frontier line upon which the soul stands. It is the necessity of life for man to journey backward into the past for food and seed with which to sow the unconquered future. For each individual yesterday holds the beginnings of art and architecture. Yesterday holds the beginnings of reform and philanthropy. Yesterday contains the rise and victory of freedom. Yesterday holds the first schoolroom and college and library. Yesterday holds the cross and all its victories over ignorance and sin. Yesterday is a river pouring its rich floods forward, lending majesty and momentum to all man's enterprises. Yesterday is a temple whose high domes and wide walls and flaming altars other hands and hearts have built. For the individual, memory is a granary for mental treasure; and, for the race, civilization is a kind of social memory.

Consider the task laid upon memory. The activity and fruitfulness of the human mind are immeasurable. Reason does not so much weave thoughts as exhale them. Objects march in caravans through the eye gate and the ear gate, each provoking its own train of thought. And the unconscious processes of the mind are of even greater number. The silent songs that genius hears, the invisible pictures that genius paints, the hidden castles that genius builds--no building of a city without can compare for wonder and beauty and richness with the building processes of the soul within. If some angelic reporter could reduce all man's thoughts to physical volume, how vast the book would be! Thoughts do not go single, but march in armies. Feelings and aspirations move like flocks of caroling songsters. Desires swarm forth from the soul like bees from a hive. The soul is a city through whose gates troop innumerable caravans, bearing treasure within, carrying treasure forth without. No Great Eastern ever carried a cargo that was comparable for vastness and richness with that voyaging forward in the mind.

Now the power and skill of God is nowhere more manifest than in this. He has endowed the mind with full power to carry forward all its joys, its friendships and victories. It is given to man to journey in a single summer over that pathway along which the human race has walked. For happiness and culture the traveler lingers by some Runnymede or Marston Moor; stays by castle or cathedral, remains long in gallery or museum. It is the necessity of his body for the traveler to leave the mountain behind him when he returns to the city in the plain. But it is the privilege of the mind to take up these sights and scenes and carry them away as so much treasure made portable by memory. By a secret process mountains and valleys and palaces are reduced in size, photographed and put away ready to be enlarged to the original proportions.

We have already heard of the inventor who planned an engine that laid its track and took it up again while it journeyed forward. But this mechanical dream is literally fulfilled in memory. Grown old and blind, each Milton may pass before his mind all the panorama of the past, to find the events of childhood more helpful in memory than they were in reality. Looking backward, Longfellow reflected that the paths of childhood had lost their roughness; each way was bordered with flowers; sweet songs were in the air; the old home was more beautiful than king's palaces that had opened to his manhood's touch.

Similarly, Dante, storm-beaten, harassed, weary of selfishness, voyaged and traveled into that foreign land that he called "youth." There he hid himself until the storms were passed. For him memory held so much that was bright and beautiful that it became to him a portfolio of engravings, a gallery of pictures, a palace of many chambers. Hidden therein, earth's troubles became as harmless as hail and snow upon tiled castle roofs. Men wonder oft how statesmen and generals and reformers, oppressed beyond endurance, have borne up under their burdens. This is their secret: they have sheltered themselves in the past, found medicines in memory, bathed themselves in old-time scenes that refreshed and cleansed away life's grime. From the chill of arctic enmity, it is given to the soul through memory to rise above the storm and cold and in a moment to enter the tropic atmosphere of noble friendship, where are fragrance and beauty, perpetual warmth and wealth.

It was a favorite principle with Socrates that the lesser man never comprehends the latent strength in his reason or imagination until he witnesses its skill in the greatest. He implies that the eloquence, art, and skill that crown the children of genius exist in rudimentary form in all men. In order, therefore, to understand memory in its ordinary processes, let us consider its functions in those in whom it is unique. Fortunately scholars in every age have preserved important facts concerning the power of recollection. The classic orators contain repeated reference to traveling singers, who could recite the entire Iliad and Odyssey. In his "Declamations," speaking of the inroads disease had made upon him, Seneca remarks that he could speak two thousand words and names in the order read to him, and that one morning he listened to the reading of two hundred verses of poetry, and in the afternoon recited them in their order and without mistake.

Muretus remarks that the stories of Seneca's memory seemed to him almost incredible, until he witnessed a still more marvelous occurrence. The sum of his statement is that at Padua there dwelt a young Corsican, a brilliant and distinguished student of civil law. Having heard of his marvelous faculty of memory a company of gentlemen requested from him an exhibition of his power. Six Venetian noblemen were judges, though there were many other witnesses of the feat. Muretus dictated words, Latin, Greek, barbaric, disconnected and connected, until he wearied himself and the man who wrote them down, and the audience who were present. Afterward the young man repeated the entire list of words in the same order, then backward, then every other word, then every fifth word, etc., and all without error.

Sir William Hamilton says that the librarian for the Grand Duke of Tuscany read every book and pamphlet in his master's library and took a mental photograph of each page. When asked where a certain passage was to be found, he would name the alcove, shelf, book, page containing the passage in question. Scaliger, the scholar, who has been called the most learned man that ever lived, committed the Iliad to memory in three weeks and mastered all the Greek poets in four months. Ben Jonson could repeat all he had ever written and many volumes he had read, as could Niebuhr, the historian. Macaulay believed that he had never forgotten anything he had ever read, seen, or thought. Coleridge tells of an ignorant family servant, who in moments of unconsciousness through fever, recited passages of Greek and Hebrew. The explanation was that the servant had been long in the family of an old clergyman whose habit it was to read aloud the Bible in the originals.

Physicians have noted instances where a foreigner coming to this country at the age of four or five has completely forgotten his native tongue. Grown old and gray, in moments of unconsciousness through fever, the aged man has talked in the forgotten language of infancy. Our best students of mental philosophy believe that no thought or feeling, no enmity or aspiration, is ever forgotten. The sentiments written on clay harden into granite. Dormant memories are not dead. At a touch they return in their old-time power and vigor. Science tells us that the flight of a bird, the falling of a leaf, the laughter of a child, the vibration of song, changes the whole universe. The boy shying a stone from one tree to another alters the center of gravity for the earth. And if the movements of dead leaves and stones are events unchangeably written down in nature, how much more are living hopes and thoughts. The soul is more sensitive than the thermometer, more delicate than the barometer, and all its processes are registered. Thoughts are events that stain the mind through in fast colors. Did man but know it, no event falls through memory's net.

It helps us to understand the immortality of memory to notice the provision made in nature for revealing hidden facts and forces. To-day chemistry shows us how events done in darkness shall be revealed in light, and the deeds of the closet be proclaimed from the housetop. In olden times princes communicated with each other by messengers. Then it was necessary to guard against the dispatch falling into the hands of the enemy, so between the lines of the apparent message was a dispatch traced in letters as colorless as water. But when the sheet was held before the blazing fire, the secret writing appeared. Thus in the kingdom of the soul, nature has provided for causing events to stand forth from the past. Under stimulus the memory performs the most astonishing feats. Excitement is a fire that causes the dim record to stand forth in clearness.

A distinguished lawyer of an Eastern city relates that while engaged in an argument upon which vast issues depended he suddenly realized that he had forgotten to guard a most important point. In that hour of excitement his faculties became greatly stimulated. Decisions, authorities and precedents long since forgotten began to return to his mind. Dimly outlined at first, they slowly grew plain, until at length he read them with perfect distinctness. Mr. Beecher had a similar experience when he fronted the mob in Liverpool. He said that all events, arguments and appeals that he had ever heard or read or written passed before his mind as oratorical weapons, and standing there he had but to reach forth his hand and seize the weapons as they went smoking by. All public men have had similar experiences--witness the testimony of Pitt, Burke and Wendell Phillips. But what event has such power to restore the records of memory as that secret excitement when the soul is like an ambassador returned home from a foreign mission to report before the throne of God? Thus, giving in its account, what sacred stimulus will fall upon memory!

In every age poets and philosophers have made much of associations as a restorer of dim memories. Porter has a story of a dinner party in which a reference to Benedict Arnold was immediately followed by someone asking the value of the Roman denarius. Reflection shows that the question was directly suggested by the topic under discussion. Benedict Arnold suggested Judas Iscariot and the thirty pieces of silver given him, and therefore the value of the coin which he received as reward. Similarly there is a tradition that Peter's face was clouded with sorrow whenever he heard the crowing of a cock. Bulwer Lytton represents Eugene Aram as scarcely able to restrain a scream of agony when a friend chanced to drive in near the spot where in murderous hate he had struck a fatal blow.

Thus, no sin is ever buried, save as a murderer buries his victim under a layer of thin sand. But let him pass that way, and a skeleton arm starts up and points to heaven and to the evil doer. The philosopher affirms that the "memory of the past can never perish until the tree or the river or the sea" with which the dark memory is associated has been blotted out of existence. Thus, the law of association ever works to bring back the ghastly phantom, to chill the blood and sear the brain. Nothing is ever forgotten. One touch, one sight, one sound, the murmur of the stream, the sound of a distant bell, the barking of a dog in the still evening, the green path in the wood with the sunlight glinting on it, the way of the moon upon the waters, the candlestick of the Bishop for Jean Valjean, the passing of a convict for Dean Maitland, the drop of blood for Donatello--these may, through the events associated therewith, turn the heart to stone and fill the life with a dumb agony of remorse.

Moreover, Shakespeare indicates how conscience in its magisterial aspects has skill for reviving forgotten deeds. In the laboratory scientists take two glasses, each containing a liquid colorless as water and pour them together, when lo! they unite and form a substance blacker than the blackest ink. As the chemical bath brings out the picture that was latent in the photographic plate, so in its higher moods events half-remembered and half-forgotten rise into perfect recollection. History tells us of the Oriental despot who in an hour of revelry commanded his butler to slay a prophet whom he had imprisoned and bring the pale head in upon a charger. Long afterward there came a day when, sitting in the seclusion of his palace, a soldier told those around the banqueting-table the story of a wonder-worker whom he had seen upon his journey. When the banqueters were wondering who this man was, suddenly the king arose pale and trembling and cried out. "I know! It is John the Baptist whom I have beheaded; he is risen from the dead!"

This old-time story tells us that dormant memories are not dead, but are like hibernating serpents that with warmth lift their heads to strike. It fulfills, as has been said, the old-time story of the man groping along the wall until his fingers hit upon a hidden spring, when the concealed door flew open and revealed the hidden skeleton. It tells us that much may be forgotten in the sense of being out of mind, but nothing is forgotten in the sense that it cannot be recalled. Every thought the mind thinks moves forward in character, even as foods long forgotten report themselves in flesh and blood. Memory is a canvas above and the man works beneath it. Every faculty is a brush with which man thinks out his portrait. Here and now, deceived by siren's song, each Macbeth thinks himself better than he is. But the time comes at last when memory cleanses the portrait and causes his face to stand forth ineffaceable in full revelation.

But memory also hath aspects gracious and most inspiring. "I have lived well yesterday," said the poet; "let to-morrow do its worst." To this sentiment the statesman added: "I have done what I could for my fellows, and my memories thereof are more precious than gold and pearls." Thus all they who have loved wisdom and goodness will find their treasures safe in memory's care. Perhaps some precious things do perish out of life. The melody trembling on the chords after the song is sung sinks away into silence. The light lingering in the clouds after the day is done at last dies out in darkness. But as the soul is consciously immortal through personality, it has an unconscious immortality through its tool or teaching, through its example or influence. Time avails not for destroying. God and the soul never forget.

Wisdom comes to all young hearts who as yet have no past, before whose feet lies the stream of life, waiting to bear them into the future, and bids them reflect that maturity, full of successes, is only the place where the tides of youth have emptied their rich treasures. He whose yesterday is full of industry and ambition, full of books and conversation and culture, will find his to-morrow full of worth, happiness and friendship. But he who gives his memory no treasure to be garnered, will find his hopes to be only the mirage in the desert, where burning sands take on the aspect of lake and river. Wisdom comes also to those who in their maturity realize that the morrow is veiled in uncertainty, and their tomb is not far distant. It bids them reflect that their yesterdays are safe, that nothing is forgotten; that no worthy deed has fallen out of life; that yesterday is a refuge from conflict, anxiety and fear.

To patriot and parent, to reformer and teacher, comes the inspiring thought that God garners in His memory every helpful act. No good influence is lost out of life. Are David and Dante dead? Are not Tennyson and Milton a thousandfold more alive to-day than when they walked this earth? Death does but multiply the single voice and strengthen it. God causes each life to fulfill the legend of the Grecian traveler, who, bearing homeward a sack of corn, sorrowed because some had been lost out through a tiny hole; but, years afterward, fleeing before his enemies along that way, he found that the seed had sprung up and multiplied into harvests for his hunger. Thus yesterday feeds in each pilgrim heart the faith that goodness shall triumph. For memory that is little in man is large in God. The Infinite One forgets nothing save human frailty and sin. Remembering the great mind, the eloquent tongue, the large purse, God remembers also the cup of cold water, and causes the humblest deed to follow its doer unto the heavenly shores.

THE IMAGINATION AS THE ARCHITECT OF MANHOOD

"Imagination rules the world."--Napoleon.

"The imagination is the very secret and marrow of civilization. It is the very eye of faith. The soul without imagination is what an observatory would be without a telescope."--Beecher.

"In such natures the imagination seems to spire up like a Gothic cathedral over a prodigiously solid crypt of common sense, so that its lightness stands secure on the consciousness of an immovable basis."--Lowell.

"Man's reason is overhung by the imagination. It rains rich treasures for fertilizing the barren soul."--Anon.

"By faith Abraham went forth, not knowing whither he went."--Hebrews.

VII

THE IMAGINATION AS THE ARCHITECT OF MANHOOD

Measured by whatsoever standard, Moses was the one colossal man of antiquity. It may be doubted whether nature has ever produced a greater mind. When we consider that law, government and education took their rise in his single brain; when we remember that the commonwealths of to-day rest upon foundations reared by this jurist of the desert; when we recall his poetic and literary skill, Moses stands forth clothed with the proportions and grandeur of an all-comprehending genius. His intellect seems the more titanic by reason of the obstacles and romantic contrasts in his career. He was born in the hut of a slave, but so strikingly did his genius flame forth that he won the approbation of the great, and passed swiftly from the slave market to the splendor of Pharaoh's palace.

Fortunately, his youth was not without the refinements and accomplishments of the schools. For then Egypt was the one radiant spot upon earth. At a time when Greece was a den of robbers and Rome was unheard of, Memphis was gloriously attractive. Schools of art and science stood along the banks of the Nile. From Thebes Pythagoras carried mathematics into Greece. From Memphis Solon derived his wise political precepts. In Luxor, architecture and sculpture took their rise. From Cleopatra's kingdom men stole the obelisks now in New York and London. Moses' opportunities were fully equaled by his energy and ambition to excel. Even in his youth he must have been renowned for his administrative genius.

But his moral grandeur exceeded his mentality. When events compelled a choice between the luxury of the court and the love of his own people, he did not hesitate, for he was every inch a hero. In that crisis he forsook the palace, allied himself with his enslaved brethren, and went forth an exile of the desert. Nor could any event be more dramatic than the manner of his return to Pharaoh's palace. Single-handed, he undertook the emancipation of a nation. Our leaders, through vast armies, achieved the freedom of our slaves; this soldier, single-handed, freed three millions of bondsmen. Other generals, with cannon, have captured castles; this man beat castles down with his naked fists. And when he had achieved freedom for his people he led them into the desert, and taught the crude and servile slaves the principles of law, liberty and government. Under his guidance the mob became an army; the slaves became patriots and citizens; the savages were clothed with customs and institutions. His mind became a university for millions. And from that day until now the columns of society have followed the name of Moses, as of old the pilgrims followed the pillar of cloud by day and the pillar of fire by night. Greater name history does not hold, save only the Name that is above every name.

Wise men will ask, where were the hidings of this man's power? Whence came his herculean strength? Moses was the father of a race of giants. He was the representative of brave men in every age, who have laid foundations upon which others have builded; he was the prototype of noble leaders who have scattered everywhere the seeds of civilization, and left others to reap the harvests; he was the forerunner of innumerable reformers and inventors, to whom it was never given to enter into the fruit of their labors; of soldiers and heroes who perished on the scaffold that others might be emancipated; of men like Huss and Cranmer, whose overthrow and defeat paved the way for others' victories. Dying, no other man has left behind influences that have wrought so powerfully or so continuously through the centuries. But when we search out the springs of his power we are amazed at his secret. We are told that he endured his tremendous burdens and achieved the impossible through the sight of the invisible. The sense of future victory sustained him in present defeat. Through the right use of the vision faculty he conquered.

Imagination was the telescope by which he saw victory afar off. Imagination was the tool with which he digged and quarried his foundations. Imagination was the castle and tower under which he found refuge from the storms, attacks and afflictions of life. No wing ever had such power for lifting, no spring ever had such tides for assuaging thirst. He bore with savages, because afar off he saw the slaves clothed with the qualities of patriots. He endured the desert, because imagination revealed a fruitful land flowing with milk and honey. He survived lawlessness, because he foresaw the day of law and liberty. He bore up under weight of cares, discouragements and responsibilities heavy enough to have crushed a score of men, because he foresaw the day of final triumph. Of old, when that legendary hero was in the thick of his fight against his enemies, an invisible friend hovered above the warrior, handing forth spear and sword as they were needed. So for the great jurist imagination reached up even into the heavenly armory and plucked such weapons as the hero needed.

Our intellectual tread will be firmer if we define the imagination and consider its uses. The soul is a city; and the external senses are gateways through which sweep all the caravans of truth and beauty. Through the eye gate pass all faces, cities and landscapes. Through the ear gate pass all sweet sounds. But when the facts of land and sea and sky have reported themselves to the soul, reason sweeps these intellectual harvests into the granary of memory for future sowing. But these harvests must be arranged. In the Orient the merchant who keeps a general store puts the swords and spears upon one shelf; the tapestries and rugs upon another; the books and manuscripts upon a third; and each thing has its own shelf and drawer. So judgment comes in to sort knowledges, and puts things useful into one intellectual shelf, things beautiful upon another shelf, and puts things true apart by themselves.

Afterward when the under-servant, called reason, has accumulated the materials, when memory has taken care of them, and judgment has classified all, then the constructive imagination comes in to create new objects. Working in iron and steel, the imagination of Watt organizes an engine; working midst the colors beautiful, the imagination paints pictures; working upon marble it carves statues; working in wood and stone it rears cathedrals; working in sound it creates symphonies; working with ideas it fashions intellectual systems; working in morals it constructs ethical principles; working toward immortality, it bids all cooling streams, fruitful trees, sweet sounds, all noble friendships, report themselves beyond the grave. For faith itself is but the imagination allied with confidence that God is able to realize man's highest ideals. Imagination therefore is a prophet. It is a seer for the soul. It toils as artist and architect and creator. It plants hard problems as seeds, rears these germs into trees, and from them garners the ripe fruit. It wins victory before battles are fought. Without it, civilization would be impossible. What we call progress is but society following after and realizing the visions, plans and patterns of the imagination.

Now our busy, bustling age is inclined to under-estimate the imagination.

Men cavil at castle-building. The pragmatist jeers at reveries. Men believe in stores, and goods in them; in factories, and wealth by them; men believe in houses and horses, but not in ideals. Nevertheless, thoughts and dreams are the stuff out of which towns and cities are builded. We may despise the silent dreamer, but in the last analysis he appears the real architect of states! Immeasurable the practical power of the vision faculty! The heroes of yesterday have all been sustained--not by swords and guns, but by the sight of the invisible!

Here is the old hero in his dungeon in Florence. While he dozed, the night before he was to be burned, the jailer saw a rare, sweet smile upon his face. "What is it?" the guard asked. "I hear the sounds of falling chains, and their clangor is like sweet music in my ears." Then, with smiling face he went to his martyrdom. And here is Michael Angelo. Grown old and blind, he gropes his way into the gallery of the Vatican, where with uplifted face his fingers feel their way over the torso of Phidias. Lingering by him one day the Cardinal Farnese heard the old sculptor say: "Great is this marble; greater still the hand that carved it; greatest of all, the God who fashioned the sculptor. I still learn! I still learn!" And he too went forward sustained by his vision of perfect beauty.

And here is John Huss, looking between the iron bars of his prison upon an army of pikes and spears, massed before his jail; but the martyr endured his danger by the foresight of the day when the swords then wielded for repression of liberty of thought would flash for its emancipation. And here is Walter Scott ruined by the failure of his publishers, just at the hour when nature whispered that he had fulfilled his task and earned his respite. But he girded himself anew for the battle, and sustained his grievous loss through the foresight of the hour when the last debt would be paid and his again would be a spotless name. And here is that youth, Emerson, looking out upon a world full of noise and strife, full of the cries of slaves and the warfare of zealots. He was sustained by the foresight of a day when God would breathe peace o'er all the scene. With hope shining in his face, he began to "take down men's idols with such reverence that it seemed an act of worship." And what shall we more say? By the sight of the invisible, Dante endured his scaffold; the heroes, hunted like partridges upon the mountains, endured their caves and the winter's cold; martyrs endured the scourge and fagot. In every age, the great, by the sight of the invisible, have been lifted into the realms of tranquillity. Outwardly, there may have been the roar and boom of guns, but inwardly men were lutes with singing harps. As the householder sitting by his blazing hearth thinks not of the sleet and hail falling on the roof of slate, so the soul abides in peace over which has been reared the castle and covert of God's presence.

How signal a place does the imagination hold in the realm of science and invention! Reason itself is only an under-servant. It has no creative skill. Memory makes no discoveries. But the imagination is a wonder-worker. One day, chancing upon a large bone of the mammoth in the Black Forest, Oken, the German naturalist, exclaimed: "This is a part of a spinal column." The eyes of the scientist saw only one of the vertebr? but to that one bone his imagination added frame, limb and head, then clothed the skeleton with skin, and saw the giant of animals moving through the forest. In that hour the imagination wrought a revolution in the science of anatomy. Similarly, this creative faculty in Goethe gave botany a new scientific basis. Sitting in his favorite seat near the castle of Heidelberg one day, the great poet was picking in pieces an oak leaf. Suddenly his imagination transformed the leaf. Under its touch the central stalk lifted itself up and became the trunk of the tree; the veins of the leaf were extended and became boughs and branches; each filament became a leaf and spray; the imagination revealed each petal and stamen and pistil, as after the leaf type, and gave a new philosophy to the science of herbs and shrubs. When a pistachio tree in Paris with only female blossoms suddenly bore nuts, the mind of a scientist suggested that some other rich man had imported a tree with male flowers, and careful search revealed that tree many miles away.

And in every department of science this faculty bridges over chasms between discovered truths. Even Newton's discovery was the gift of imagination. When the eyes of the scientist saw the falling apple it was his vision faculty that leaped through space and saw the falling moon. When the western trade winds, blowing for weeks, had cast the drift wood upon the shores of Spain, Columbus' eyes fell not only upon the strange wood but also upon a pebble caught in the crevice. But his imagination leaped from the pebble to the Western continent of which the stone was a part, and from the tree to the forest in which it grew.

This faculty has performed a similar work in the realm of mechanics. Watt tells us that his engine worked in his mind years before it worked in his shop. In his biography, Milton recognizes the beauty of the trees and flowers he culled from earth's landscapes and gardens, but in his "Paradise Lost," his imagination beheld an Eden fairer than any scene ever found on earth. Napoleon believed that every battle was won by the imagination. While his soldiers slept, the great Corsican marshaled his troops, hurled them against the enemy, and won the victory in his mind the night before the battle was fought. Even the orator like Webster must be described as one who sees his argument in the air before he writes it upon the page, just as Handel thought he heard the music falling from the sky more rapidly than his hand could fasten the notes upon the musical bars. Thus every new tool and picture, every new temple or law or reform, has been the imagination's gift to man.

Nor has the case been different with men in the humbler walks of life. Multitudes are doomed to delve and dig. Three-fourths of the race live on the verge of poverty. The energies of most men are consumed in supporting the wants of the body. It is given to multitudes to descend into the coal mine ere the day is risen, to emerge only when night has fallen. Other multitudes toil in the smithy or tend the loom. The division of labor has closed many avenues for happiness and culture. The time was when the village cobbler was primarily a citizen, and only incidentally a shoemaker. In the old New England days the cobbler owned his garden and knew the orchard; owned his horse and knew the care of animals; had his special duties in relation to school and church, and, therefore, was a student of all public questions. But tending a machine that clinches tacks, cabins and confines the soul. The man who begins as a citizen ends an appendage to a wheel. The life of many becomes a treadmill existence. Year in and year out they tend some spindle. Now this drudgery of modern life threatens happiness and manhood. Therefore it was ordained that while the hand digs the mind may soar.

While Henry Clay's hands were hoeing corn in that field in Kentucky, through his imagination the young orator was standing in the halls of Congress. What orations he wrote! What arguments he fashioned! Each time his hoe cut down a weed, his mind with an argument hewed down an opponent. Never was there a tool for hoeing corn like unto the imagination! Christine Nilsson tells that once she toiled as a flower girl at the country fairs in Sweden. But all the time she delved she was dreaming, and by her very dreams making herself strong against the day when she would charm vast audiences with celestial music. What battles the plowboys have fought in dreams! What orations they have pronounced! What reforms they have achieved! What tools invented! What books written! What business reared! Thus the imagination shortens the hours of labor and sweetens toil. While the body tires, the soul soars and sings.

This young foreigner newly arrived in our city digs downward with his spade, but his imagination works upward into the realm of the invisible. He endures the ditch and the spade through foresight of the day when his playmate will come over the sea; when together they will own a little house, and have a garden with vines and flowers, with a little path leading down to "the spring where the water bubbles out day and night like a little poem from the heart of the earth;" when they will have a little competence, so that the sweet babe shall not want for knowledge. By that dream the youth sustains his loneliness and poverty; by that dream he conquers his vices and passions; at last through that dream he is lifted up to the rank of a patriot and worthy citizen. Nor shall you find one hard-worked man caught to-morrow in life's swirl who does not endure the strife, the rivalry and the selfishness of the street with this gift divine. It is the noblest instrument of the soul. Thereby are the heavens opened. Imagination is the poor man's friend and saviour. Imagination is God whispering to the soul what shall be when time and the divine resources have accomplished their work upon man.

And when imagination has achieved for man, his progress, happiness, and culture, it goes on to help him to gain personal worth and character. Above every noble soul hangs a vision of things higher, better and sweeter. It causes the best men even in their best moods to feel that better things still are possible. By sweet visions it tempts men upward, just as of old the bees were lured onward by the honey dropped through the hunter's hands. The vision of a higher manhood discontents men with to-day's achievement and takes the flavor out of yesterday's victory. In such hours it is not enough that men have bread and raiment, or are better than their fellows. The soul is filled with nameless yearnings and longings. The deeper convictions, long hidden, begin to stir and strain, even as in June the seed aches with its hidden harvest.

Though the youth still pursues, he never overtakes his ideal. In the process of transmutation into life the ideal is injured and dwarfed. Just as the poet's vision is transcendently more beautiful than the song he writes upon the page; as the artist's dream is a glorious-creation, but his picture is only a photograph thereof; as the musician's song or symphony is but an echo of the ethereal music he heard in his soul, so every purpose and ideal is marred in the effort to give it expression and embodiment.

These children of aspiration hold the secret of all progress for society. Just as of old artists drew the outline of glowing and glorious pictures, and then with bits of colored glass and precious stones filled up the mosaic, causing angels and seraphs to stand forth in lustrous beauty, so imagination lifts up before the youth its glowing plans and purposes, and asks him to give himself to the details of life in filling it up and perfecting a glorious character. The patterns of life are only given upon that holy mount where, midst clouds and darkness, dwell God and the higher imagination.

But if the imagination has its use, it has its abuse also. If visions of truth and beauty can exalt, visions of vice can debase and degrade. In that picture where Faust and Satan battle together for the scholar's soul, the angels share in the conflict. Plucking the roses of Paradise, they fling them over the battlements down upon the heads of the combatants. When the roses fall on Faust they heal his wounds; when they fall on Satan they turn into coals of fire. Thus the imagination casts inspirations down upon the pure, but smites the evil into the abyss. The miseries of men of genius like Burns are perpetual warnings to youth against the riotings of imagination. There are poems, also novels and lurid scenes in the city, hanging pictures before the imagination and scorching the soul like flames of fire. For as of old so now, what a man imagineth in his heart that he is. For not what a man does outwardly, but what he dreams inwardly, determines his character.

Most men are better than we think, but some men are worse. As steam in the boiler makes itself known by hisses, so the evil imaginings heave and strain, seeking escape. Many forbear vice and crime through fear; their conscience is cowardice; if they dared they would riot through life like the beasts of the field; if all their inner imaginings were to take an outward expression in deeds, they would be scourges, plagues and pests. In the silence of the soul they commit every vice. But they who sow the wind shall reap the whirlwind; the revealing day will come when the films of life shall be withdrawn, and the character shall appear faithful as a portrait, and then all the meanness and sliminess shall be seen to have given something to the soul's picture. Oh, be warned against these dreams, all ye young hearts! The indulgence of the imagination is like the sultriness of a summer's day; what began so fair ends with sharp lightnings and thunder. How terrible is this word to evil-doers! "As a man thinketh in his heart, so is he."

It is also given to this vision faculty to redeem men out of oppression and misfortune, and through its intimations of royalty to lend victory and peace. Oft the days are full of storms and turbulence; oft events grow bad as heart can wish; full oft the next step promises the precipice. There are periods in every career when troubles are so strangely increased that the world seems like an orb let loose to wander widely through space. In these dark hours some endure their pain and trouble through dogged, stoical toughness. Then men imitate the turtle as it draws in its head and neck, saying to misfortune: "Behold the shell, and beat on that." But, God be thanked! victory over trouble has been ordained. In the blackest hour of the storm it is given to the vision faculty to lift man into the realm of tranquillity. As travelers in the jungle climb the trees at night and draw the ladder up after them, and dwell above the reach of wild beasts and serpents, so the soul in its higher moods ascends into the realms of peace and rest. In that dark hour just before Jesus Christ entered into the cloud and darkness, and fronted His grievous suffering, He called His disciples about Him and uttered that discourse beginning: "Let not your hearts be troubled." Strange wonder words; words of matchless genius and beauty.

Moreover, the vision faculty furnishes man his idea and picture of God. Many suppose that all that is necessary to understand the divine nature is that it should be stated distinctly in language. Greater error there could not be. There can be no language for causing a little child to understand the larger truths of heroism, art or government. The unripe cannot understand the mature. Each mind must paint its own picture of God. Nature itself is but a palette upon which God draws her portrait. Reason furnishes the materials and truths about God, and the imagination unites them in some noble conception of His all-helpful nature. Everything in nature that has power or beauty or benefit has received it from God. Moving along the Alpine valleys the traveler sees huge bowlders lying in the stream, and, looking to the mountain side, his eye rests upon the very cliff from which the bowlder fell. Thus discerning the noble qualities in mother or patriot, in hero or friend, we trace their beautiful qualities back to God, from whom all noble souls borrow their excellence. In the largest sense all the elements of power in sea and sky and sun, all the beauty of the fields and forests, of summers and winters, are letters in nature's alphabet for spelling out the name of God. As a diamond has many facets, and every one reflects the sun, so the universe itself is a gem whose every facet reflects the mind and genius of God.

When reason has culled out of life and nature everything that excites awe or admiration, everything that represents bounty and beauty, then imagination lifts up all these ideals and sweeps them together and melts them into one glowing and glorious conception of the God of power, wisdom and love. But even then the heart whispers: "He is that, and infinitely more than that, even as the sun is more than the little taper man has made." But if the reason and memory, through misuse, furnish but few of the truths about God, and if the imagination has been weakened in its power, then how poor the picture the soul paints!

What scant, feeble portraits of God some men have! What can an Eskimo, whose highest conception of summer is a stunted bush, know of tropical orchards, of luscious peach, pear and plum? If the student has seen only the broken fragments of Phidias, what can he know of the Parthenon as it once stood in the zenith of its perfection, in the splendor of its beauty? But if man's reason can cull out all the lustrous facts of nature and history, and if his imagination has strength and skill to bring them all together, then how beautiful will be the face and name of God! That name will fill his soul with music. That thought will set his heart vibrating with tumultuous joy. If all the air were filled with invisible bells, and angels were the ringers, and music fell in waves as sweet as melted amethyst and pearl, we should have that which would answer to the sweetness that by day and night rains down upon the hearts of those who approach God--not through the eye nor ear, not through argument nor judgment, but through the heart, through the imagination, as they endure, beholding Him who is invisible.

THE ENTHUSIASM OF FRIENDSHIP

"He that walketh with wise men shall be wise."--Solomon.

"The only way to have a friend is to be one."--Emerson.

"A talent is perfected in solitude; a character in the stream of the world."--
G 鯀 the.

"It is certain that either wise bearing or ignorant carriage is caught as men take diseases, one of another; therefore let men take heed of their company."--Shakespeare.

"Beyond all wealth, honor or even health, is the attachment we form to noble souls, because to become one with the good, generous and true, is to become, in a measure, good, generous and true ourselves."--Thomas Arnold.

"Cicero said: 'Friendship can make riches splendid.' Friendship can plan many things for its wealth to execute. It can plan a good winter evening for a group, and it can plan an afternoon for a hundred children. It can roll in a Christmas log for a large hearth. It can spread happiness to the right and left. It can spend money most beautifully and make gold to shine. Civilization itself is of the heart."--Swing.

VIII

THE ENTHUSIASM OF FRIENDSHIP

Destiny is determined by friendship. Fortune is made or marred when the youth selects his companions. Friendship has ever been the master-passion ruling the forum, the court, the camp. The power of love is God-breathed, and life has nothing like love for majesty and beauty. Civilization itself is more of the heart than of the mind. As an eagle cannot rise with one wing, so the soul ascends borne up equally by reason and affection. Plato found the measure of greatness in a man's capacity for exalted friendship. All the great ones of history stand forth as unique in some master passion as in their intellectual supremacy. Witness David and Jonathan, with love surpassing the love of women. Witness Socrates and his group of immortal friends. Witness Dante and his deathless love for Beatrice. Witness Tennyson and his refrain for Arthur Hallam. Witness the disciples and Christ, with "love as strong as death."

Sweetness is not more truly the essence of music than is love the very soul of a deep, strong, harmonious manhood. Friendship cheers like a sunbeam;

charms like a good story; inspires like a brave leader; binds like a golden chain; guides like a heavenly vision. To love alone is it given to wrestle victoriously with death.

Lord Bacon said: "He who loves solitude is either a wild beast or a god." The normal man is gregarious. He wants companionship. The very cattle go in herds. The fishes go in shoals. The bees go in swarms. And men come together in families and cities. As men go up toward greatness their need of friendship increases. No mind of the first order was ever a hermit. Modern literature enshrines the friendships of the great and makes them memorable. While letters last, society will never forget Charles Lamb and his companions; Dr. Johnson and his immortal group; Petrarch and his helpless dependence upon Laura; while the letters of Abnard and Heroise enshrine them in everlasting remembrance.

In all literature there is no more touching death-bed scene than that of the patriarch Jacob. Dying, the Prince forgot his gold and silver, his herds and lands. Lifted up upon his pillows, in tremulous excitement he took upon his lips two names--God and Rachel. More than a score of years had passed since her death, but in that memorable hour the great man built a monument to her who had fed his joy and deepened his life.

Friendship carries a certain fertilizing force. All biographers tell us that each epoch in a hero's life was ushered in by a new friend. When Schiller met Goethe every latent talent awakened. The poet's friendship caused the youth to grow by leaps and bounds. Once, returning home after a brief visit to Goethe's house, one exclaimed: "I am amazed by the progress Schiller can make within a single fortnight!" Perhaps this explains why the great seem to come in groups. Thrust an Emerson into any Concord, and his pungent presence will penetrate the entire region. Soon all who come within the radius of his life respond to his presence, as flowers and trees respond with boughs brilliant and fragrant to the sunshine when spring replaces the icy winter. After a little time, each Emerson stands girt about with Hawthornes, Whittiers, Holmeses, and Lowells. The greatness of each Milton lingers in his friends, Cromwell and Hampden, as the sun lingers in the clouds after the day is done. Therefore the great epics and dramas, from the Iliad to the Idylls of the King, are stories of friendships. Take love out of our greatest literature, and it is like taking a sweet babe out of the clothes that cover it. Man listens eagerly to tales of eloquence and heroism, but loves most of all the stories of the heart. God is not more truly the life of dead matter than is love the very life of man.

Now, the secret of eminence in the realm of industry or art or invention is this: that the worker has wrought in his luminous mental moods. In its passive, inert states, the mind is receptive. Then reason is like a sheathed sword. Thought must be struck forth as fire is struck from flint. But under inspirational moods the mind begins to glow and kindle. Then the reason of the orator, the poet or reformer ceases to be like a taper, needing a match to light it, and becomes a sun, blazing with its own radiance. Spencer wrote: "By no political alchemy can we get golden conduct out of leaden instincts." Thus there is no necromancy by which the mind can get superior work out of its inferior moods.

When, then, reason approaches its task under the inspiration of enthusiasm and love, nature yields up all her secrets. Here is the author sitting down to write. Memory refuses facts, and reason declines to create fictions. The mind is dull and dead. Suddenly the step of some friend long absent is heard at the door. Then how do the faculties awake! Through all the long winter evening, the mind brings forth its treasures of wit, of anecdote, of instructive fact and charming allusion. Here is some Edison, with an enthusiasm for invention, who found his electric lamps that burned well for a month had suddenly gone out, and read in the morning paper the judgment of the scientist that his electric bulb was a good toy but a poor tool.

In his enthusiasm for his work, the man exclaimed, "I will make a statue of that professor, and illumine him with electric lamps, and make his ignorance memorable." Then Edison went away to begin a series of experiments that drove sleep from his eyes and slumber from his eyelids through five successive days and nights, until love and enthusiasm helped reason to wrest victory from defeat.

Here is the boy Mozart, with his love of music, toiling through the long days at tasks he hated, and in the darkening twilight stealing into the old church, where he poured out his very soul over the organ keys, sobbing out his mournful melodies. Here is Lincoln, with his enthusiasm for books, coming in at night all aching with cold and wet, and rising when parents slept, to roll another log upon the blazing hearth, while midst the grateful heat his eager eyes searched out the treasures that lay along the line of the printed page, until his mind grew rich and strong. And here are the Scottish clansmen and patriots, for love's sake, following the noble chieftain, their hearts all aflame, who, if they had a hundred lives, would gladly have given them all for their heroic leader. And here is the orator rising to plead the cause of the savage, and of the slave, before men who feel no sympathy, and are as castles locked and barred. But the love for the poor shines in Wendell Phillips' eyes, trembles in his voice, pleads in his thinking, until the multitude become all plastic to his thought, and his smile becomes their smile, his tear their tear, the throb of his heart the throb of the whole assembly. Here is the Scottish girl, in love with truth, standing midst the sea, within the clutches of the incoming tide. She is bound down midst the rising waters. Doomed is she and soon must die. But her eyes are turned upward toward the sky, and a great sweet light is on her face that tells us enthusiasm and love in her have been victorious over death. Truly, that Greek did well to call enthusiasm "a god within," for love is stronger than death.

The historian tells us that all the liberties, reforms and political achievements of society have been gained by nations thrilling and throbbing to one great enthusiasm. The Renaissance does not mean a single Dante, nor Boccaccio, but a national enthusiasm and a "god within all minds." The Reformation is not a single Savonarola, nor Luther, but a universal enthusiasm and "a god within," all heart and conscience. If we study these movements of society as typified by their leaders, these heroes stand forth before us with hearts all aflame and with minds that grow like suns. In times of great danger men develop unsuspected physical strength, and the force of the whole body seems to rush upward and compact itself with the thumb or fist. And in the mental world lawyers and orators tell us that at heated crises, when great issues hang upon their words, the memory achieves feats otherwise impossible. In these hours the mind becomes luminous. All the experience of the past passes before the orator with the majesty of a mighty wave or a rushing storm. Similarly, the hero inflamed with love or liberty becomes invincible. When some Garibaldi or Lincoln appears, and the people behold his greatness and beauty and magnanimity, every heart catches the sacred passion. Then the narrow-minded youth tumbles down his little idols, sets up diviner ideals, and finds new measurements for the thrones of heaven and earth. Then, in a great abandonment of love, the nation pours out its heart for the cause it loves.

Froude tells us that self-government has cost mankind hundreds of wars and thousands of battle-fields. Tennyson writes of the boy who was following his father's plow when the share turned up a human skull. There, where the plow stayed, the patriot had fallen in battle. Sitting upon the furrow with the child upon his knee, the father caused his boy to see a million men in arms fighting for some great principle; to see the battle-fields all red with blood; the hillsides all billowy with graves; caused him to hear the shrieking shot and shell; pointed out the army of cripples hobbling homeward. When the child shivered in fear the father whispered, "Your ancestors would have gladly died daily for the liberty they loved." And if to-day good men brood over the wrongs of Armenia, and breathe a silent prayer for those who struggle against desperate odds and "the unspeakable Turk," and if to-morrow and on the morrow's morrow editors and orators unite in words of sympathy and encouragement for the patriots fighting in some Cuba, it is because we believe the love of liberty implies the right to liberty; that despotism corrupts manhood; that self-government is the best for industry, the best for integrity, the best for intelligence. If the red plowshare of war must pass through the soil of the nations, may it bury forever the seeds of oppression and injustice, and sow for future generations the seeds of liberty, intelligence and religion!

Moreover, an overmastering passion is the secret of all eminence in scholarship. Each autumn the golden gates of learning swing wide to welcome the thousands who enter our colleges and universities. If it were possible for each young student to sit down and speak with the library and laboratory as with a familiar friend, we would hear wisdom's voice uttering one report: "I love them that love me." None of those forms of mental wealth called art or science or literature, enters the mind unasked or stays unurged. All the shelves are heavy with mental treasure, but only the eager mind may harvest it. Beauty sleeps in all the quarries, but only the eager chisel wakens it. Wealth is in every crack and crevice of the soil, but nature forbids the sluggard to mine it. Those forms of paradise called fame, position, influence, stand with gates open by day and night, but the cherubim with flaming swords wave back all idle youth. When the Grecian king set forth upon his expedition he stayed his golden chariot at the market-place. Lifting up his voice he forbade any man's body to enter his chariot whose heart remained behind. Thus the mind is a chariot that sweeps no unwilling student upward toward those heights where wisdom and happiness dwell.

To-day our young men and women stand in the midst of arts, vast, beautiful and useful; they are surrounded by all the facts of man's marvelous history; they breathe an atmosphere charged with refinement. But the youth who hates his books might as well be the poor savage lying on the banks of the Niger, whose soul sits in silence and starves to death in a silent dungeon. Should a kind heaven give us the power to select some charmed gift to be dropped down upon our youth, parents and teachers could ask nothing better than that each young heart should storm the gates of learning with such enthusiasm as belonged to Milton or Epictetus. The Roman slave had one leg broken and twisted by a cruel master, but in his enthusiasm for knowledge he used the dim light of his cell for copying the thoughts of great authors, and lay awake at night reflecting upon the problems of life and death with man's mysterious nature, and so made himself immortal by his devotion to the truth. For the student, enthusiasm is indeed "a god within." Ignorance is want of mental animation. The scientist tells us the Patagonians sleep eighteen hours each day, with a tendency to doze through the other six. Their minds are unable to make any kind of movement, and the chief once told Sir John Lubbock that he would love to talk were it not that large ideas made him very sleepy.

But it is all in vain that man has reason or learning or imagination if these talents lie sleeping. Not long ago the ruins of an old temple were discovered in Rome. When the spade had turned up the soil, lo, seeds long hidden awakened to cover the soil with rich verdure. For 2,000 years these germs had slept, waiting for the day of warmth and quickening. Thus each faculty of man is latent, until some powerful enthusiasm passes over it. Indeed, mental power is not in the multitude of knowledge acquired, but in the powerful enthusiasms that drive the informed soul along some noble path. Power is not in the engine, but in the steam that pounds the piston; and the soul is a mechanism driven forward by those motives called enthusiasm for learning or influence or wealth. Success might be defined as a full casting of the heart into some worthy cause.

It is high time that our young men should recognize that prosperity and wealth are won only when the mind moves enthusiastically along the pathway of industry. Our young men have been deeply injured by the fact that now and then some one stumbles upon sudden wealth, or by accident gains great treasure. But for every one such fortunate person, there are ten thousand who have failed of success for want of a purposeful enthusiasm.

The Persians have a strange story of the Golconda diamond mines. Once Ali Hafed sat with his wife looking out upon the river that flowed through their farm. Soon their children came through the trees bringing with them a traveler. In confidence the stranger showed Ali Hafed a diamond that shone like a drop of condensed sunshine. He told his host that one large diamond was worth whole mines of copper and silver; that a handful would make him a prince; that a mine of diamonds would buy a kingdom. That night wealthy Ali Hafed went to bed a poor man, for poverty is discontent. When the morning came he sold his farm for gold, and went forth in search of diamonds. Years passed. Old and gray he returned in rags and poverty. He found his dear ones had all died in penury. He also found that the peasant who bought his farm was now a prince. One day, digging in the white sand in the stream at the foot of the garden, the peasant saw a shining something that sent his heart to his mouth. Running his hands through the sand, he found it sown with gems. Thus were discovered the Golconda mines. Had Ali Hafed dug in his own garden, instead of starvation, poverty and a broken heart, he would have owned gems that made nations rich.

This legend reminds us how youth constantly throws away its opportunities. Each day some man exchanges a farm in Pennsylvania for the prairies of Dakota, only to find that the hills he despised have developed oil that makes his successor rich. Each year purposeful men grow rich out of trifles that the careless cast away. The sewers of Paris have made one man wealthy with treasure beyond that of gold mines. The wastes of a cotton mill founded the fortune of one of the greatest families in England. Peter Cooper used to say that he built the Cooper Institute by picking up the refuse that the butcher shops threw aside. A boy tugging over a shoe-last in Haverhill, Mass., was told by his mother to give himself to making better and stronger lasts. Twenty years of enthusiastic study ended, and he was president of one of the greatest of our railways. In 1870, a youth sat upon the slag heap of a mine in California. But he gave his full mind to each clod, and going away for a few weeks he returned with a machine that extracted greater treasure from the slag than men had ever gained from the mines. All wise men unite in telling us that ours is a world where prosperity is won by fidelity to details, and that wealth comes through little improvements. But, best of all, a purposeful enthusiasm gives mental wealth, and achieves a treasure beyond gold and rubies--a worthy character.

Nor is there any dross that love will not refine away, nor any vice that love can not expel from the heart. Wordsworth was so impressed with the evil of avarice that he could compare it only to a poisoned vine that wrapped itself so tightly about his favorite tree that vine and tree became one life, and the removal of the one meant the death of the other. But in her most famous story George Eliot tells us that avarice passes utterly away before the touch of love. Silas Marner was the victim of blackest ingratitude. His friend was a thief, who thrust upon him the blame of a black crime. Suddenly, this innocent man found all homes closed to his hand, all shops locked to his tools, while even the market refused his wares. Through two years and more, right bravely he held his head aloft and looked all men in the face. At length hunger and want drove him forth a wanderer. Then he shook off the dust of his feet against his false friends, and cursed their firesides. Kindness in him soured into cynicism, his sweetness became bitterness, his faith in God and man fluttered feebly for awhile, then lay without a single pulse-beat. In anger he cursed God, but could not die.

Journeying afar, the traveler at length stayed his steps in a distant village. Then in toil he sought to forget. Rising a great while before day, he wrought with the activity of a spinning insect; and while men slept, his loom hummed far into the night. When fifteen years had passed, he had much gold and was a miser. Under the brick floor he secreted his treasure. Each night he locked the door, shuttered his windows, and poured upon the table his gold and silver. He bathed his hands in the yellow river. He piled his guineas up in heaps. Sometimes he slept with arms around his precious money-bags. One evening he lifted the bricks of the floor, to find that the hole was empty. Benumbed with terror, he went everywhither seeking his treasure. He kneaded his bed, swept his oven, peered into each crack and crevice. When the full truth fell upon the miser, he sent forth a wild, ringing scream--the soul's cry of desolation. Then in his grief he rushed into the rain and the wild night, and wandered on and on, stupefied with pain. Not until morning came did he stagger in out of the storm. Entering, he saw the glint of yellow by his hearth. With a wild cry he sprang forward and clutched it. But it was not gold; it was something better--it was the yellow locks of a sleeping child. Brokenhearted, with nothing else to live for, Silas Marner took the deserted babe into his bosom. As the weeks went on, the little creature nestled into his heart. For the child's sake he turned again to his loom; love taught him thrift and industry. For the child's sake he bought books and hived knowledge; love made a scholar of him. For the child's sake he planted vines, roses and all sweet flowers; love made him an artist. For the child's sake he bought carpets for the bare floors and pictures for the wall; love had made him generous. For the child's sake he knelt one night and recited her prayer; love would fain make him a Christian. But he hated men, and could not forget their ingratitude. One day a rich man's carriage stopped before his cottage. The lord of the mansion told a strange story--how this beautiful girl of eighteen was his daughter. In that hour the girl, tall and beautiful, turned away from palace, lands, position, and, for the love she bore him, put her arms around Silas Marner and refused to leave him. Then something in him gave way, and Silas Marner wept. Then confidence in man and God was his again. Love had destroyed avarice and purged away his sin. For love is a civilizer; it makes saints out of savages. As an armor of ice melts before the sun, so all vice and iniquity disappear in the presence of an overmastering affection.

It remains for us to consider that the absence of an enthusiastic devotion to integrity and the law of God explains the moral disasters and shipwrecks that have increased the tears and sorrows of mankind. Recently the people of this land opened their morning papers only to be deeply shocked by a rehearsal of grievous disasters, not all of which were physical. It seems that an awful cyclone had swept through a Western community, twisting the orchards, destroying houses and barns, and leaving behind a swath wide and black with destruction. In addition, the foreign news told of a volcano whose crater had suddenly poured forth a river of lurid lava, which, sweeping down the mountain side, consumed the homes of the flying multitude. But the saddest disaster was reserved to the last. It told of the shame and sorrow, from which there is no recovery, that had befallen the parents and friends of three young men, hitherto held in high honor. It seems that for many years these men had been honored by their friends, and trusted by the banks in which they were employed. But in a dark hour they determined to cease to be gentlemen, preferring, rather, to join the ranks of thieves. Despising every principle of honor, the gold which employers committed to their care was taken, not to the safety vault, but distributed among gamblers and evil persons. And our heavy sorrow is increased when we read in our commercial reports that last year 625 men went astray as embezzlers, robbing the people in forty-five states of $25,234,112. The time seems to have come for this nation to sit down in sackcloth and ashes.

To all good men comes the reflection that either this immorality must cease its ravages, or this nation will be irretrievably disgraced. Were it possible to search out these unhappy men, some of them wearing the convict's garb, and some wandering as fugitives in foreign lands, henceforth to be men "without a country," and question each for the cause of his deep disgrace, from all would come this shameful confession: "I loved evil and hated the law of God." Not one could confess to passionate, enthusiastic devotion to the divine laws. But every tree not rooted goes down before the storm, and every ship unanchored midst the rocks will go to pieces when the wind rises. Would that we could to-day cause the laws of God to stand forth as sharply defined as mountain peaks before the eyes of all young men; would that we could also kindle in each a passionate love and loyal affection for these holy laws. If the youth of to-day are to be the leaders of to-morrow, and are ever to have power to stir their fellows, to correct abuses, revolutionize society, or organize history, they must, with the enthusiasm of love, ally themselves with God and His law, clothing that law with flesh until it becomes visible, clothing it with voice until it becomes eloquent, thrilling it with power until it becomes triumphant. Only love fulfills law!

Most of all does man need the enthusiasm of love toward his God and Saviour. In the olden time Plato expressed a wish to have the moral law become a living personage, that beholding, mankind might stand amazed and entranced at her beauty. The philosopher felt that abstractions were too cold to kindle the soul's enthusiasm. As planets are removed from the sun, their light and heat lessen; their flowers fade; their fruits lack luster; their summers shorten. Thus Neptune stands in the midst of perpetual ice and winter, without tree or bird or human voice. But as our earth approaches the direct rays of the sun, its beauty increases, its harvests grow heavy.

As if to fulfill Plato's desire, Jesus Christ drew near to our world, not to chill man's heart, but to strengthen his affection, refine his reason, enlarge his horizon. How admirable Christ's words, how illustrious His work, how divine His character! The philosopher describes man, but Jesus Christ loves man, weeps for man, dies for man. Dante inspires, but Jesus Christ gives life.

Shakespeare shines, but Jesus Christ uplifts. History causes the heroes of yesterday to pass before the mind, surrounded by applauding multitudes. When Napoleon entered Paris the people ran together with one accord, and the tides of enthusiasm rose like a mountain freshet. When Garibaldi entered Florence, when Kossuth passed up Broadway in New York, when Grant, returning homeward, entered our own city, the streets were filled solidly with multitudes who forgot hunger and exhaustion, exalted by hero-worship.

But the divine man never stood forth in full proportion until Jesus Christ stepped upon this planet. What strength! What gentleness! Behold His exquisite sympathy! Behold the instinct of confidence, that drew little children to His arms! How did men, defiled within and without, throng round Him, while His presence wrought the miracle of miracles in cleansing them! Then for the first time in history did disheveled ones so feel the beauty of goodness that an irresistible enthusiasm drew them about Him to kiss the very hem of His garment. All the excellencies of life, and more, unite in Him; the orator's persuasive speech; the artist's love of beauty; the scholar's passion for truth; the patriot's love of country. His also is more than the love of mother, lover, friend, for his is the love of Saviour. To-day He rises over each soul in such majesty of excellence as to include the excellencies of everything in heaven and everything on earth. As the clouds sometimes, after hanging for days and nights in the atmosphere, at length come together and pour down their refreshing showers, so let all that is deepest and richest and sweetest in man's thought and affection pour itself out before Him who is worthy of the world's anthem. For His mind will guide, His mercy forgive, His love redeem, His hand lead--not into the abyss of death, but unto the heavenly heights. He who with Dante looks upward to-day may behold the Saviour's divine chariot "sweeping along the confines of heaven, a sweet light above it, its wheels almost blocked with flowers."

CONSCIENCE AND CHARACTER

"There is a higher law than the constitution."--Seward.

"Whatever creed be taught, or land be trod, Man's conscience is the oracle of God." --Byron.

"Labor to keep alive in your breast that little spark of celestial fire called conscience."--Washington.

"Trust that man in nothing who has not a conscience in everything."--Sterne.

"If you can find a place between the throne of God and the dust to which man's body crumbles, where the fatal responsibilities of law do not weigh upon him, I will find a vacuum in nature. They press upon him from God out of eternity and from the earth out of nature, and from every department of life, as constant and all-surrounding as the pressure of the air."--Beecher.

IX

CONSCIENCE AND CHARACTER

Von Humboldt said that every man, however good, has a yet better man within him. When the outer man is unfaithful to his deeper convictions, the hidden man whispers a protest. The name of this whisper in the soul is conscience. And never had monarch aspect so magisterial as when conscience terrified King Herod into confession. The cruel, crafty despot had slain John the Baptist to gratify the revenge of the beautiful Jezebel, his wife, reproved of John for her outrageous sins. But soon passed from memory that hateful night when the blood of a good man mingled with the red wine of the feast. Luxury by day and revelry by night caused the hateful incident to be forgotten. Soon a full year had passed over the palace with its silken seclusion. One day, when the dead prophet had long been forgotten, a courtier at the king's table told the story of a strange carpenter, whose name and fame were ringing through the land.

Who is He? asked the feasters, pausing over their spiced wine. Who is He? asked the women, gossiping over the new sensation. Suddenly, conscience touched an old memory in Herod's heart. In terror the despot rose from the banquet. As in the legend, when the murderer's finger touched the gaping wound the blood began again to flow--a silent witness against the unsuspected but guilty friend, so Herod's conscience opened up again his guilty secret. Memory, thrusting a hooked pole into "the ocean of oblivion, brought up the pale and drowned deed." The long-forgotten sin was revealed in all its ghastly atrocity. It availed nothing that Herod was a Sadducee--the agnostic of antiquity. For, when conscience spake, all his doubts fell away.

Immortality and responsibility were clear as noonday. Holding a thousand swords in her hand, conscience attacked the guilty king. Then were fulfilled Plato's words: "If we could examine the heart of a king, we would find it full of scars and black wounds." For no slave was ever marked by his master's scourge as Herod's heart was lashed by his conscience.

Socrates told his disciples that the facts of conscience must be reckoned with as certainly as the facts of fire or wood or water. None may deny the condemnation that weighed upon the soul of Herod or Judas, or the approval of conscience that transfigured the face of the martyred Stephen or Savonarola. For all happiness comes only through peace with one's self, one's record, and one's God. All the great, from 苊 chylus and Sophocles to Channing and Webster, have emphasized man's conscience as the oracle divine. Let the witnesses speak. Here is the Judge, famous in English history: It became his duty to sentence a servant for murdering his master. Suddenly, before the astounded onlookers, the Judge arose and took his place in the dock beside the prisoner. He stated that, thirty years before, in a distant province, he had taken the life and property of his master, and thereby gained his present position and influence. Though he had never been suspected of crime, he now begged his fellow Judges to condemn him to the death unto which his conscience had long urged him. Here is the student of man and things, Dr. Samuel Johnson: In his old and honored age he goes back to Litchfield to stand with uncovered head from morning till night in the market-place on the spot where fifteen years before he had refused to keep his father's book-stall. Despite the grotesque figure he made, midst the sneers and the rain, conscience bade him expiate his breach of filial piety. And here is Channing, the scholar and seer: A child of six years, he lifted his stick to strike the tortoise, as he had seen older boys do. But in that moment an inner voice whispered loud and clear: "It is wrong." In his fright the boy hastened home to fling himself into his mother's arms. "What was the voice?" he asked. To which his mother answered: "Men call the voice conscience; but I prefer to call it the voice of God. And always your happiness will depend upon obedience to that little voice."

Here also is the great Persian Sadi. One day he found a good man in the jungle, who had been attacked by a tiger and horribly mutilated. Despite his dreadful agony, the dying man's features were calm and serene. "Great God," said he, "I thank thee that I am only suffering from the fangs of the tiger and not of remorse." And here is Professor Webster, endungeoned for the murder of Dr. Parkman. One morning he sent for his jailer and asked to be placed in another cell. "At midnight," he said, "the prisoners in the next cell tap on the wall and whisper, 'Thou art a murderer.'" Now there were no prisoners in the next cell. The whispers were the echoes of a guilty conscience.

Daniel Webster also testifies: Once he was asked what was the greatest thought that had ever occupied his mind. "Who are here?" "Only your friends." Then this colossal man answered: "There is no evil we can not face or flee from but the consequences of duty disregarded. A sense of obligation pursues us ever. It is omnipresent like the Deity. If we take to ourselves wings of the morning and dwell in the uttermost parts of the sea, duty performed or duty violated is still with us, for our happiness or our misery. If we say that darkness shall cover us, in the darkness as in the light, our obligations are yet with us. We can not escape their power nor fly from their presence. They are with us in this life, will be with us at its close, and in that scene of inconceivable solemnity which lies yet farther on we shall find ourselves followed by the consciousness of duty--to pain us forever if it has been violated, and to console us so far as God has given us grace to perform it." Weighed against conscience the world itself is but a bubble. For God himself is in conscience lending it authority.

We also owe the great dramatists and novelists a debt, in that they have portrayed and analyzed the essential facts of man's moral life. That which Shakespeare does for us in "Macbeth," Victor Hugo does in his "Les Miserables." The latter work, always ranked as one of the seven great novels, exhibits happiness and character as fruits of obedience to the soul's inner circle. Jean Valjean was an escaped convict. Going into a distant province he assumed a new name and began life again. He invented a machine, amassed wealth, became mayor of the town, was honored and beloved by all. One evening the good mayor heard of an old man in another town who had been arrested for stealing fruit. The officer apprehending him perceived in the old man a striking resemblance to Jean Valjean. Despite his protests he was tried as Jean Valjean, and was about to be remanded to prison--this time for life. Unless some one cleared him he must go to the galleys. Only Jean Valjean himself can clear the stranger. How clear him? By confessing his identity and going himself.

In that hour the mayor's brain reeled. He retired to his inner room. Then the tempest raged in his brain as a cyclone rages through the trees, twisting off the branches and pulling up the roots. Must he go back again to the galleys with their profanity and obscenity? Must he resign his mayoralty and his wealth? Must he give up his life, so useful and helpful, and all to save a possible year or two of life for this old man? Were not these two young wards whom he was supporting more than this one old wreck? Fate had decided. Let the old man go to the galleys.

Then with muscles tense as steel, with jugular vein all swollen and purple, Jean Valjean took the two candlesticks given him by the Bishop, his thorn cane, the coin taken from the boy, and cast all upon the blazing coals. Soon the flames had licked all up. Then Victor Hugo says: "Jean Valjean heard a burst of internal laughter." What was it in him jeering and mocking? At midnight from sheer exhaustion the mayor slept. Dreaming, he seemed to be in a hall of justice where an old man was being tried. There were roses in the vase, only sin had bleached the crimson petals gray. The sunlight came through the window, only sin had washed the color from the sunbeam and left the golden rays ashen pale. All the people were silent. At length an officer touched the mayor and said: "Do you know you have been dead a long while? Your body lives, but you died when you slew your conscience." Suddenly a voice said: "Jean Valjean, you may melt the candlestick, burn your clothes, change your face, but God sees you." Afterward came a second burst of internal laughter. Then the mayor arose swiftly, took his horse, drove hard all night and reached the distant village to enter the courtroom just as the old man was about to be sent to the galleys. Ascending the prisoner's dock, he confessed his identity. Victor Hugo tells us that in that hour the judge and the lawyer saw a strange light upon the mayor's face, and felt a light within dazzling their hearts. It was the same light that fell on the German monk's face when before the Emperor at Worms he said: "I cannot and will not recant!" and then boldly fronted death. Conscience shining through made Luther's face luminous, as it had made the face of Moses before him!

As obedience to the behests of conscience has always yielded happiness and formed character, so disobedience has always destroyed manhood. The great novelists have exhibited the deterioration of character in their hero as beginning with a sin against the sense of duty. In Romola, George Eliot exhibits Tito as a gifted and ideal youth. The orphan child was adopted by the Greek scholar, who lavished upon him all the gifts of affection, all the culture and embellishments of the schools, all the comforts of a beautiful home; and when the longing for foreign travel came upon the youth the foster-father could not deny him, but took passage for Tito and himself and sailed for Alexandria. But the motto of Tito's life was, get all the pleasure you can, avoid all the pain. Soon the old scholar became a clog and a burden. One night, conscience battled for its life with Tito. At midnight the youth arose, unbuckled from his father's waist the leather belt stuffed with jewels, and fled into the night, leaving the gray-haired man among strangers whose language he could not speak.

Then this youth sailed away to Florence. There his handsome person, his Southern beauty, his grace of address, his aptitude for affairs, won him the admiration of the wisest statesmen and the heart of one of the noblest of women. But all the time we feel toward this beautiful youth that same loathing and contempt that we feel toward a beautiful young tiger. Tito had no conscience toward Romola, no conscience toward her father's priceless library, no conscience toward the patriots struggling for the city's liberty; he played the traitor toward all. His soul was, indeed, sheathed in a glowing and beautiful body; but it was the corpse sheathed over with flowers and vines; and so conscience becomes an avenger upon Tito. When the keystone goes from the arch, all must crash down in ruins. Unconsciously but surely the youth moved toward his destruction. The day of doom was delayed, but there came an hour when conscience first drove Tito into the Arno's swift current, and then became a millstone, that sunk him into the deep abyss. For ours is a world in which nature and God cannot afford to permit sin to prosper. Conscience is God's avenger.

Open all the master books, and they portray the same truth. Three of the seven greatest novels deal with conscience. Seven of the world's greatest dramas are studies of conscience and of duty. The masterpieces of Sophocles and Achylus, of Dante and Milton, of Goethe and Byron, are all studies of the soul's oracle, that, disobeyed, hurls man into the abyss, or, followed, becomes wings, lifting him into the open sky.

Demosthenes said that knowledge begins with definition. What, then, is conscience? Many misconceptions have prevailed. Multitudes suppose it to be a distinct faculty. The eye tests colors for beauty, the ear tests sounds for harmony, the reason tests arguments for truth, and there is a popular notion that conscience is a distinct faculty, testing deeds for morality. Many suppose that, when God made man, He implanted conscience as an automatic moral mechanism, a kind of inner mind, to act in his absence; but conscience is not a single faculty. It includes many faculties, and is complex in nature. It has an intellectual element, and this is distinctly fallible and capable of education. Witness the Indians, believing it to be right to kill aged persons. Witness savages of old, sacrificing their children to appease the gods. Just as there has been an evolution in tools, in laws and in institutions, so has there been an evolution of the intellectual element in conscience. Thucydides tells us that the time was in Sparta when stealing was right. In that far-off time a boy was praised for exhibiting skill and dexterity in pilfering. Stealing was disgraceful and wrong only when it was found out, and, if the theft was large and skillfully done, it won honor--a condition of things that still prevails in some sections.

Never since man stepped foot upon this planet has there been a time when conscience, the judge, has praised a David when sinning against what he believed to be the law of right; never once has it condemned a Daniel in doing what he believed to be right. In this sense conscience is, indeed, infallible and is the very voice and regent of God.

Since, therefore, conscience partakes of this divine nature and speaks as an oracle, what are its uses and functions? Primarily, the moral sense furnishes a standard and tests actions for righteousness or iniquity. To its judgment-seat comes reason, with its purposes and ambitions. When his color sense is jaded the artist uses the sapphire or ruby to bring his tints up to perfection. And when contact with selfishness or sordidness has soiled the soul's garments, dulled its instruments, and lowered its standards, then conscience comes in to freshen the ideals and to smite vice and vulgarity. In these luminous hours when conscience causes the deeper convictions to prevail, how beautiful seem truth and purity and justice! How does the soul revolt from iniquity, even as the eye revolts from the slough or the nostril from filth!

Conscience has also relations to judgment. It pronounces upon the inner motive that colors the deeds, for it is the motive within that makes the actions without right or wrong. When Coleridge, the schoolboy, was going along the street thinking of the story of Hero and Leander and imagining himself to be swimming the Hellespont, he threw wide his arms as though breasting the waves. Unfortunately, his hand struck the pocket of a passer-by and knocked out a purse. The outer deed was that of a pickpocket and could have sent the youth to jail. The inner motive was that of an imaginative youth deeply impressed by the story he was translating from the Greek, and that inner motive made the owner of the purse his friend and sent young Coleridge to college. Thus, the philosopher tells us, the motive made what was outwardly wrong to be inwardly right.

Memory, too, is influenced by the moral Faculty. Memory gathers up all our yesterdays. Often her writing is invisible, like that of a penman writing with lemon juice, taking note of each transgression and recording words that will appear when held up to the heat of fire. Very strangely does conscience bring out the processes of memory. Sir William Hamilton tells of a little child brought to England at four years of age. When a few brief summers and winters had passed over his head, the language of far-off Russia had passed completely out of the child's mind. Seventy years afterward, stricken with his last illness, in his delirium the man spoke with perfect ease in the language of childhood. In moments of extreme excitement, when ships go down or death is imminent, conscience doth so quicken the mind that all the deeds and thoughts of an entire career are reviewed within a few minutes. Scholars have been deeply impressed with this unique fact. Seeking to interpret it, Walter Scott takes us into the castle where a foul murder was committed. So deeply did the red current stain the floor that, though the servants scrubbed and scrubbed and planed and planed, still the dull red stains oozed up through the oaken planks. This is the great Scotchman's way of saying that our deeds stain through the very fiber and substance of the soul.

Looking backward, we see only here and there a peak of remembrance standing out midst the sea of forgetfulness, even as the islands in the West Indies stand out midst the ocean. But each of these island peaks represents a submerged continent. Drain off the sea, and the mountains ease off toward the foothills and the hills toward the great plains that make up the hidden land. Thus the isolated memories of the past are all united, and will at length stand forth in perfect revelation. Verily, conscience is a witness, secretly taking notes, even as good Latimer in his cell overheard the scratching of the pen in the chimney behind the curtain. Conscience is a judge, and, though juries nod and witnesses may be bribed, conscience never slumbers and never sleeps. Conscience is a monarch, and, though to-day the soul's king be deposed from its throne, to-morrow it will ascend to the judgment-seat and lift the scepter. For conscience represents God and acts in His stead.

Consider the workings of conscience in daily life. The ideal man is he who is equally conscientious toward intellect and affection, toward plan and purpose. But in practical life men are Christian only in spots and departments. The soul may be likened unto a house, and conscience is the furnace thereof. Sometimes the householder turns the heat into the sitting-room and parlor, but in the other rooms he turns off the warm currents of air. Sometimes heat is turned into the upper rooms, while the lower rooms are cold. Thus conscience, that should govern all faculties alike, is largely departmental in its workings. Some men are conscientious toward Sunday, but not toward the week days. On Sunday they sing like saints, on Monday they act like demons. On the morning of St. Bartholomew's massacre, Charles IX was conscientious toward the cathedral and attended mass during three hours; in the evening he filled the streets of Paris with rivers of blood. John Calvin was conscientious toward his logical system. He was very faithful to his theology, but he had no conscience toward his fellows, and burned Servetus without a sympathetic throb.

In the Middle Ages conscience worked toward outer forms. In those days the baron and priest made a contract. The general led his peasants forth to burn and pillage and kill, and the priest absolved the murderers for five per cent of the profits. Men were very conscientious toward absolution, but not at all toward the neighbor's flocks and barns. In others conscience is largely superstition. Recently an officer of our army found himself sitting beside his host at a table containing thirteen guests. The soldier, who perhaps would have braved death on the battle-field, was pricked by his conscience for sitting at table where the guests numbered thirteen. But he was afraid to die at the dinner-table. He believed that the great God who makes suns and stars and blazing planets to fly from His hand as sparks beneath the hammer of a smith, the god of Sirius and Orion, always stopped his work at six o'clock to count the guests around each table, and if he found perchance there were thirteen, then would lift his arrow to the bow to let fly the deadly shaft upon these awful sinners against the law of twelve chairs or fourteen.

Singularly enough, now and then an individual is conscientious toward some charm, as in the case of a merchant who presently discovered that he had left his buckeye at home. He had carried this for twenty years. Had he forgotten to pray he would not have gone home to fall upon his knees. Nature and God were in the merchant's counting-room, but not the buckeye. So he hurriedly left his office to bring back the agent that secured all his success and prosperity.

Then, there is a commercial conscience. Some men feel that the law of right is chiefly binding upon a man in his business relations. They exile themselves from home, break the laws of love and companionship with the wife whom they have engaged to cherish and love, until they become strangers to her. But conscience does not prick them. Home, friends, music, culture, all these may be neglected--but the business, never. Others there are whose consciences work largely toward the home. When they cross their own thresholds they are genial, kind and delightful. As hosts they are famed for their companionship. Dying, their fame is gathered up by the expressions, "good husband, good father, good provider." But they have no conscience toward the street. They count other men their prey, being grasping, greedy and avaricious. They feel about their fellows just as men do about the timber in the forest. When a man wants timber for his house, he says, "That is the tree I want," and the woodsman fells it and squares it for the sill. Does he want stone for his foundations or marble for his finishings? There are the rocks; quarry them. Men go into inanimate nature and get the materials they need. Nor is it very different in the great world of business and ambition. The giant takes one man for the foundation and cuts him down and builds him into the walls; he selects another man and uses him up, building his substance into the structure; he looks upon his fellows as the shepherd upon his flocks--so much wool to be sheared.

Nor is the work of conscience very different in the moral and spiritual realm. Here is one man who is conscientious toward yesterday. Ten years ago, he says, "while kneeling in the field light broke through the clouds" and he obtained "a hope." And every Sunday since that day he has not failed to recall that scene. He is not conscientious about having a new, fresh, crisp, vital experience for to-day, but he is conscientiously faithful in recalling that old experience. It is all as foolish as if he should say that ten years ago he had a bath, or ten years ago he drank at the bubbling spring, or ten years ago he met a friend. What about to-day's purity, to-day's loaf and to-day's friendships? The heart should count no manna good that is not gathered fresh each morning. Others there are whose conscience works largely toward doctrine and intellectual statements. With them Christianity is a function of thought in the brain. These are they who want every sermon to consist of linked arguments. The good deacon sits in his pew and listens to the unfolding of proofs of election or foreordination. When the arguments have been piled up to sixteen or eighteen, the good man begins to chuckle with delight, saying, "Verily, this is a high day in Israel; my soul feasts on fat things." Other men want some flesh on their skeletons, but he is fed on the dry bones of logic.

Sometimes conscience affects only the feelings. Fifty years ago there was a type numbering hundreds of thousands of persons whose religion was largely emotional. In great camp-meetings filled with a warm atmosphere men showed at their best. The sunny spot of all the year was the month of revival meetings. Then they experienced the luxury of spiritual enjoyment. They lived on the top of some Mount of Transfiguration, while the world below was thundering with wickedness and tormented with passion. Men became drunk with emotions. Religion was an exquisite form of spiritual selfishness. Afterward came an era when men learned to transmute feelings into thoughts and fidelities toward friendships and business and duty. At other times conscience has had unique manifestations in fidelity toward creeds. Now one denomination and now another, forgetting to be conscientious in meeting together for days and weeks to plan in the interests of the pauper, the orphans, the tenement house or the foreign district in the great city, will through months of excitement exhibit conscience toward some doctrinal symbol. Witness the recent upheaval about inspiration. As water bubbling up through the spring was once rain that fell from the sky, so the truth coming through the lips of poet or prophet was first breathed into the heart by God. Recently a good professor thought more emphasis should be laid upon the human spring. But his opponents thought the emphasis should be placed upon the sky, from which the rain fell. In the broil about the nature of the water, the spring itself was soiled, much mud stirred up, until multitudes wholly forgot the spring, and many knew not whether there was any water of life.

But conscience in some, means fidelity to what man and God did--not what

God is doing or will do. When the flowing sap under the stimulus of the sun causes the tree to grow and splits the bark, men rejoice that the bark is rent and that new and larger growths must be inserted. Sometimes a child, long feeble and sickly, enters upon a period of very rapid growth. Soon the boy's old clothes are too small, and so is his hat. But what if the parents should remember only that the clothes and hat came from some famous pattern? What if in their zeal to preserve the hat they should put an iron band about the boy's forehead and never permit it to increase so that the hat would not fit? What if they should put a strait-jacket about the chest to restrain the stature? This would show great zeal toward the hat and the coat, but meanwhile what is to become of the boy? Strange that men should be so conscientious toward an intellectual symbol, but forget to give liberty to other men's consciences who day and night seek to please God and be true to their beliefs. Thus in a thousand ways conscience is partial and fragmentary in its workings. Only one full-orbed man has ever trod our earth!

God's crowning gift to man is the gift of conscience. Reason is a noble and kingly faculty, turning reveries into orations and conversations into books. Imagination is a stately and divine gift, turning thoughts into poems and blocks of stone into statues. Great is the power of an eloquent tongue instructing men, restraining, inspiring, stimulating vast multitudes. Great are the joys of memory, that gallery stored with pictures of the past. But there is no genius of mind or heart comparable to a vigorous conscience, magisterial, clear-eyed, wide-looking. He who gave all-comprehending reason, all-judging reason, reserved his best gift to the last--then gave the gift of conscience.

Man is a pilgrim and conscience is the guide, leading him safely through forests and thickets, restraining from the paths of wrong, pointing out the ways of right. Man is a voyager and conscience is his compass. The sails may be swept away, and the engines stopped, but the voyager yet may be saved if only the compass is kept. In time of danger man may be careless about his garments, but not about his hand or foot or eye. It is possible to sustain the loss of wealth, friends and outer honors, but no man can sustain the loss of conscience. It is the soul's eye. Afar off it sees the face of God. Instructed, guided, loved, and redeemed by Jesus Christ, he who while living is at peace with his Master and with his conscience will, when dying, find himself at peace with his God.

VISIONS THAT DISTURB CONTENTMENT

"Like other gently nurtured Boston boys, Wendell Phillips began the study of law. Doubtless the sirens sang to him, as to the noble youth of every country and time. Musing over Coke and Blackstone, perhaps he saw himself succeeding Ames and Otis and Webster, the idol of society, the applauded orator, the brilliant champion of the elegant ease, and the cultivated conservatism of Massachusetts. * * * But one October day he saw an American citizen assailed by a furious mob in the city of James Otis for saying with James Otis that a man's right to liberty is inherent and inalienable. As the jail doors closed upon Garrison to save his life, Garrison and his cause had won their most powerful and renowned ally. With the setting of that October sun, vanished forever the career of prosperous ease, the gratification of ordinary ambition, which the genius and the accomplishments of Wendell Phillips had seemed to foretell. Yes, the long-awaited client had come at last. Scarred, scorned and forsaken, that cowering and friendless client was wronged and degraded humanity. The great soul saw and understood."-- Oration on Wendell Phillips by George Wm. Curtis.

X

VISIONS THAT DISTURB CONTENTMENT

Every community holds a few happy and buoyant souls, that are so sustained by inner hope and outer prosperity as to seem the elect children of good fortune. These are they who are born only to the best things, for whom, as life goes on, the years do but increase happiness and success. For other men happiness is occasional, and life offers now and then a bright interval, even as an open glade is found here and there in the dark forest. Among these sunny souls, dwelling midst constant prosperity, let us hasten to include that youth to whom Christ made overtures of friendship. His was a frank and open nature, his a fresh and unsullied heart. He had also a certain grace and indescribable charm that clothed him with rare attraction. Wealth, too, was his, and all the advantages that go therewith. Yet ease had not enervated him, nor position made him proud. He had indeed passed through the fierce fires of temptation, but had come out with spotless garments.

Beholding him, Christ loved him; nor could it have been otherwise. Some men we force ourselves to like. For reasons of finance or social advantage, men ignore their faults, while cherishing a secret dislike. But others are so attractive, they compel our friendship by a certain sweet necessity. The eye must needs like the rich red rose, and the ear can not but enjoy the sweet song. And this youth stood forth clothed with such rare attraction that it is said Christ cast one long lingering look of affection upon him; then widening the circle of friendship, he offered the young ruler a place therein. It was an overture such as Socrates made to the boy Plato; it was a proffer such as Michael Angelo made to the poor young artist who knocked at his door. Recalling the day when he met Goethe, Schiller was accustomed to say his creative literary career began with Goethe's proffer of friendship.

Carlyle tells us that each new epoch in his life began with the acquaintance of some great man. For it is not given to books nor business, to landscapes nor clouds nor forests, to have full power over the living man. Only mind can quicken mind, only heart can quicken heart. What would the youth of genius not give for the friendship of some Bacon or Shakespeare? But when this youth won Christ's regard, it was as if all the children of genius had come together in Christ's single person, to proffer intimacy and companionship. His great soul overhung his friends as the harvests overarch the fields, "filling the flowers with heat by day, and cooling them with dews by night." His friendship is like a mother's, a lover's, a friend's, but larger than either, and deeper than all. The rising of a star, that glows and sparkles with ten thousand effects, can alone be compared to this Son of Man, who flamed forth upon his friends such majesty of beauty, such royalty of kindling influences.

For centuries scholars have spoken of this interview between Christ and the young ruler as "the great refusal." Dante, wandering with Virgil through the Inferno, thought he saw this young ruler searching for his lost opportunity. For this ruler was the Hamlet of the New Testament. Like the Prince of Denmark, he stood midway between his conscience and his task, and indecision slew him. It has been said that Hamlet could have been happy had he remained in ignorance of his duty, or had he boldly obeyed the vision which called him to action. It was because he knew more than he had the courage to do that a discord arose, which destroyed the symmetry and sanity of his mind. His madness grew out of the breach between his enlarged and haunting sense of right and his faltering ability to face and fulfill it. Thus also the tragedy of this young ruler's life grew out of the fact that the new aspiration made his old contentment impossible, and compelled him either to go on with boldness to better things, or to go back to emptiness and misery. Beholding him, Christ loved him for what he was, and pointed out what he might become. He knew that the better was a great enemy of the best. For Christ had the double vision of the sculptor.

Before him was the mass of marble, rude and shapeless. But the outer shapelessness concealed the inner symmetry. Only the flying chips could let loose the form of glowing beauty hidden within. And before that youth he lifted up a vision of still better things. He set the youth midway between the man he was and the man he might become. He had achieved so much that Christ would fain lead him on to perfection itself. When the husbandman beholds his vines entering into leafage and blossom, he nurtures them on into fruitage. When Arnold finds some young Stanley ready to graduate, he whispers: "One thing thou lackest; let all thy life become one eager pursuit of knowledge." And to this youth who had climbed so high came the vision of something fairer and better still.

Going on before, Christ lured him forward, even as of old the goddess lured the Grecian boy forward by rolling rosy apples along the path. But the interview ended with the "great refusal." And the youth went away, not angry nor rebellious, but sad and deeply grieved at himself. For now he knew how far his aspiration outran performance. Like Hamlet, indecision palsied action. Contentment perished, for the vision of perfection ever haunted him. At first Christ's words and look of earnest affection filled his heart with a tumult of joy: but having fallen back into the old sordid self, the very memory of his master's face became a curse and torture. And so the vision blighted that should have blessed.

Now, the lives of great men tell us that God has always used visions for disturbing contentment, destroying ease, and securing progress. Witness the life of that young patrician, Wendell Phillips. His college mates love to describe him as they first saw him in the halls of Cambridge. His elegant person, his accomplished manners, his refined scholarship, made him the idol of the Harvard boys. Even in his youthful days he excelled as an orator, and was the easy master of the platform. But to him came the sirens singing of leisure, of opulence, and ambition. Full oft he looked forward to the day when he would be the champion of "elegant repose and cultivated conservatism" of the patrician element in his patrician state. But suddenly the Christ, in the person of one of his little ones, crossed the young scholar's path. One golden October afternoon, while Wendell Phillips was sitting in his office, he heard the noise of a strange disturbance in the street. Looking out he saw the mob maltreating Garrison, as, with blows and kicks, they dragged him toward the jail. All that night young Phillips lay tossing on his couch, thinking ever of this man who had been mobbed in the city where Otis had said "Liberty of speech is inalienable."

All that night the vision of the slave, scarred and scorned and forsaken, stood before his mind, while ever he heard a voice whispering: "Inasmuch as ye have done it unto one of the least of these my brethren, ye have done it unto me." In that vision hour perished forever all his dreams of opulence and ease. He decided to turn his back upon all preferment and ambition, all comfort and leisure, and follow his vision whithersoever it led. Soon the vision led him to the platform of Faneuil Hall, where an official was justifying the murderers of Lovejoy. "Mr. Chairman," he said, "when I heard the gentleman lay down principles which placed the murderers of Alton side by side with Otis and Hancock, with Quincy and Adams, I thought those pictured lips would have broken into voice to rebuke the recreant American, the slanderer of the dead." And that vision lent his words such burning eloquence that Wendell Phillips' speech in Faneuil Hall ranks with Patrick Henry's at Williamsburg and Abraham Lincoln's at Gettysburg--and there is no fourth. His vision led him unto obloquy also. What revilings were his! What bitter hatred! What insults and scoffs! At last the vision led him unto fame. The very city that would have slain him builded his monument, and men who once would not defile their lips with his name taught their children the pathway to his tomb. It was that vision splendid that saved Phillips from sodden contentment. Had Christ never crossed his path, his imagination would have lost its brightest picture, his life its noblest impulses, its most energetic forces.

And not only have visions power to shape young men's lives. To the mature and the great also come dreams of ideal excellence, smiting selfishness, rebuking sin, taking the sweetness out of sordid success, and urging men on to higher achievements. The biographers have never been able to fully account for the pathetic sadness and gloom of the closing days of Daniel Webster. Horace Greeley once said that "Webster's intellect is the greatest emanation from the Almighty mind now embodied." For picturesque majesty and overpowering mentality he is doubtless our most striking figure. That enormous and beautiful head, those wonderful eyes, that stately carriage, that Jove-like front, led men to call him "the godlike Daniel." When he appeared upon the Strand in London a great crowd followed him, and a British statesman described Webster as one describes a majestic landscape or the sublimity of a mountain. But during the last years of his life his face took on a strangely pathetic sorrow. With the language of a Dante his biographer has pictured for us an Inferno, in which we see one, sublime of reason, walking in the very prime and strength and grandeur of full manhood, yet walking in a round of night, in a realm of bitterness, ever gnawed by disappointment and consumed by fierce ambition. He sank into his grave, says the historian, "under a heart-crushing load of political despair."

But disappointed ambition cannot account for Daniel Webster's sadness and woe. Strength was his for supporting the loss of a nomination. He knew that his title, "Defender of the Constitution," was fully equal to the title of President. He was too great a man to have his heart broken by the loss of political honor. What was his woe? Let us remember the young ruler who was sad and grieved after he met Christ, and had refused to obey the heavenly vision. Let us remember the dream that came to Pilate, and how, afterward, the great Roman was uneasy and restless. And to Daniel Webster there came the memory of his speech in favor of a law compelling men in the North to send fugitive slaves back to their masters; and there also came the words of Christ, who said: "I am come to give deliverance to the captive." And looking forward, Webster anticipated the judgment of the generations upon the breach between his duty and his performance. That vision of higher things haunted him. Oft he heaved sighs of bitter regret. Daniel Webster was saddened and deeply grieved at what he himself had done. For the hope of the Presidency he sacrificed his convictions as to the slave. The heavenly vision bade him deliver the captives, not send them back into slavery. No political disappointment crushed Daniel Webster. The consciousness of duty performed would have sustained him under any sorrow. It was the consciousness of having sinned against the heavenly vision that broke his heart, and brought Webster's gray hairs down with sorrow to the grave!

Plutarch tells us that the finest culture comes from the study of men in their best moods. But always life's best moods come through these heavenly visions. George Eliot makes the destiny of each hero or heroine to turn upon the use of those critical hours when some ideal fronts the soul for acceptance or rejection. To Maggie Tulliver came a delicious moment when her lover offered her honorable marriage, and would have led her into a perfumed garden of perfect happiness. But just in that hour when joy bubbled like a little spring in her heart, there came the memory of the crippled boy, to whom years before in her childhood she had plighted her troth. And the vision of her duty and the thought of his disappointment led her to refuse pleasure's spiced cup, and choose self-renunciation and a life for others. That heavenly vision saved her from plunging into the abyss of selfishness, even as the lightning's flash in the dark night reveals the precipice to the startled traveler.

And when the visions divine have rebuked selfishness, they go on to conquer sin. Hawthorne uses the vision for redeeming his hero. To Arthur Dimmesdale, pursued by his enemy, came the dream of freedom, when, journeying to a foreign land with Hester and Pearl, he might regain health and happiness and find peace again in walking in the dear old paths of wisdom and study. But the day before his ship sailed came the vision splendid, bidding him mount the scaffold, confess his wrong, and free his conscience of its guilt. And it was obedience thereto that redeemed his life from hypocrisy.

And, having saved men from wrong, the vision goes on to secure their service for the right. Here is that colored woman, Harriet Tubman, whom John Brown introduced to Wendell Phillips as the best and bravest person upon our continent. If Frederick Douglass wrought in the day, Harriet Tubman toiled at night; for when the man had praise and honor, the black woman had only obscurity and neglect. When this bravest of her race escaped from slavery in 1850 and reached Canada she exclaimed exultingly, "I have only one more journey to make--the journey to heaven." But in that hour when the tides of joy rose highest there came the vision calling her back to danger and service. She was not disobedient thereto, but turned her face again toward the cotton fields. Between 1850 and 1860 she made nineteen trips into the South, and rescued over three hundred slaves. One day while lying in a swamp with her band of fugitives, a black man brought her word that a reward of $40,000 had been offered by the slave dealers of Virginia for her apprehension. Hard pressed by her pursuers, she sent her fugitives on by a secret route and went herself to the train. But when she saw in the car advertisements for her arrest she left the Northern train and took the next one going south, thinking by her fearlessness to escape detection, and also to collect a new band of fugitives. And so her people came to call Harriet Tubman the Moses of the black race. And, following on, the vision lifted her to a place among those whom the world will not willingly let die.

When the vision has redeemed bad men to good deeds it goes on to redeem good ones unto perfection. Here is Channing, with his cultured scholarship, his refined manners, his gentle goodness. So heavy were the drafts study made upon his strength that at length came a day when the mere delivery of his sermons and orations left him physically exhausted. But he went smilingly and forever from the pulpit, and gave up also the use of his pen. In that hour, when sorrow and gloom rested heavily upon those who loved him, the vision shone clearly for Channing. He determined to turn his whole life into a sermon and poem. With pathetic eloquence he said, "It is, indeed, forbidden me to write or speak, but not to aspire and be. To live content with small means; to seek elegance rather than luxury, and refinement rather than fashion; to be worthy, not respectable, and wealthy, not rich; to do all cheerfully, bear all bravely; to listen to stars and birds, to babes and sages, with open heart; to study hard, think quietly, act frankly, talk gently, await occasions, hurry never--in a word, to let the spiritual, unbidden and unconscious, grow up through the common--this is to be my symphony."

Into our nation also has come the disturbing vision. Ours is called an age of unrest. We hear much about social discontent. Beneath all the outer activity and bustle there is an undertone of profound sadness. Neither wealth, pleasure, nor politics has availed to conceal the world's weariness. Strangely enough, just at a time when prosperity is greatly increased, when our homes are full of comforts and conveniences, when all the forces of land and sea and sky have lent themselves to man as willing servants, to carry his messages, run his errands, reap his harvests, pull his trains, and push his ships; in an age when a thousand instruments that make for refinement and culture have been invented, just at this time, strangely enough, unrest and disquietude have fallen upon our people. Why is our age so sad? Has Schopenhauer carried the judgment of mankind by his favorite motto, "It is safer to trust fear than faith?" Is it because our age has lost faith in God? Have doubt and skepticism burned the divine dew off the grass, and left it sere and brown? Nay, a thousand times nay!

The world is sad because it has found God, not lost him. Man is weary in the midst of his wealth and pleasures for the same reason that the young ruler was grieved and sad in the midst of his great possessions. Our age has seen the vision splendid, but halts undecided, being yet unwilling to go on and fulfill its new ideals. For those who have eyes to see, Jesus Christ stands again in the market and the street. He has given society a new vision of the earth as a possible paradise, filled with the fruits of peace and plenty where none know surfeit, and none know want. He has given a vision of the brotherhood of man and the fatherhood of God, and that vision has destroyed the old contentment. Our fathers were happy because what they did kept pace with what they saw. And we are unhappy because we are unwilling to do what we see.

This vision of possible excellence will continue to haunt our generation until performance shall have overtaken the ideal promise. All the processes of buying and selling without must be carried up to meet the requirements of the vision within. Just as in Luther's day the vision divine disturbed Germany and filled the land with unrest until the people achieved spiritual freedom; just as in Cromwell's day the vision of freedom in political relations came to England and gave disturbance until the doctrine of the divine right of kings was overthrown; just as in our own day the vision of liberty for all, without regard to race or color, disturbed our land and filled our council chambers with conflict and strife, and turned the South into one immense battle-field, until the laws of the Nation matched the ideals of God--so to-day, the vision of the brotherhood of man in Jesus Christ has fallen upon the home, the market, and the forum, and brought restlessness and discontent to our people.

Our colleges are restless, and by the university extension plans are seeking to fulfill their vision of wisdom for all. The church hath seen the heavenly vision, and, restless and grieved at its own failures, is rewriting its creeds, inventing new methods of social sympathy and social help, and is seeking eagerly to fulfill its vision. Wealth too, is discontented, and by manifold gifts is becoming the almoner of universal bounty toward school and college, and gallery and church. Looking toward the council chamber, society is becoming restless, and feeling that the council chamber should be as sacred as a temple, and that as of old so now evil men have turned the temple into a place for money-changing, and made the house of God a den of thieves. Good men are again lifting the scourge of small cords. The discontent is becoming universal. This vision of a new order will continue to haunt and disturb men, until at length society will make all its activities without correspond to the heavenly vision within.

The tradition tells us that when the young ruler who made the "great refusal" had returned home he found the old zest of life had gone. Gone forever his contentment in fields and flocks, in houses and horses and goods; in books and pictures! He himself seemed but a shadow moving through a phantom world. Struggle as he would, he could not forget the new vision, nor find the old joy. At last he ceased struggling, and, fulfilling his vision, he found the cross was the magic key that opened the door of happiness.

And to the youth of this far-off day, the vision splendid doth come again. In strange ways come these luminous hours and exalted moods. Sometimes they come through memory, and then the tones of a voice long still fall softly upon the ear like celestial bells calling us heavenward. Sometimes these luminous hours come through the affections, when anticipations of joy are so bright that it seems as if the youth reaching forward had plucked beforehand the fruit from the very tree of life. For some they come through sorrow, when the soul stands dissolved in tears, even as some perfumed shrub stands in the June morning making the very ground wet with falling raindrops. Then the soul wanders here and there, all dumb with grief, seeking comfort, yet finding none. Then sitting near the much-loved grave, the soul hears the night winds whispering, "Not here, not here!" to which the murmuring sea replies, "Not here," while the weeping vines and the mournful pines ever answer, "Not here, not here!" But softly falling through the pathless air comes a voice murmuring, "Here! Here! Come up hither!"

Oh, these luminous hours! These hours of deeper conviction are life's real hours! Summer is sunshine and beauty, not storm and snow. There are dark and wintry days in March, when spring seems a delusion. There are days in April so cold that summer seems a snare. But between the storms there are brief warm intervals when the sun falls soft on the south hillsides, and the roots begin to stir and the seeds to ache with harvests, and all the air is vocal. The fitful snows in April are but reminders of what the dying winter was; but these occasional sunny days are prophecies of what summer hath accomplished in its full ministry upon the fields and forests.

And after long periods of sodden selfishness and clouded sin, suddenly the vision of better things breaks through the cloud and storm. Then the vision strikes clarity into reason, memory and imagination. In these hours the soul scoffs at sordid things. As the flower climbs upward to escape from the slough, as the foot turns away from the mire, as the nostril avoids the filth, as the ear hates discord, so in these hours the soul scoffs at selfishness and sin. Oh, how beautiful seem purity and gentleness, and sympathy and truth! And these hours are big with prophecy. They tell us what the soul shall be when time and God's resources have wrought their will upon man. They are to be cherished as the mariner cherishes the guiding star that stands upon the horizon; they are to be cherished as some traveler, lost in a close, dark forest, cherishes the moment when the sun breaks through a rift in the clouds and he takes his bearings out of the swamp and toward his home. Visions are God within the soul. They come to lead man away from sin and sorrow. They come to guide him to his heavenly home.

THE USES OF BOOKS AND READING

"Bring with the books."--Paul.

"A good book is the precious lifeblood of a master spirit embalmed and treasured up on purpose to a life beyond life."--Milton.

"God be thanked for books. They are the voices of the distant and the dead, and make us heirs of the spiritual life of past ages. In the best books great men talk to us, give us their most precious thoughts and pour their souls into ours."--Channing.

"All that mankind has done, thought or been is lying as in magic preservation in the pages of books. They are the chosen possession of men."--Carlyle.

"We need to be reminded every day how many are the books of inimitable glory, which, with all our eagerness after reading, we have never taken into our hands. It will astonish most of us to find how much of our very industry is given to the books which have no worth, how often we rake in the litter of the printing press, whilst a crown of gold and rubies is offered us in vain."--F. Harrison.

XI

THE USES OF BOOKS AND READING

Paul was at once a thinker, a theologian, and a statesman, because he was always a scholar. One duty he never neglected--the duty of self-culture through reading. Certain companions were ever with him--his favorite authors. Imprisoned in Rome, the burden of his letters to his young friend in Ephesus was books and the duty of reading. Himself a Hebrew, by much study he became a cosmopolitan and a citizen of the wide-lying universe. Like Emerson, he believed that "the scholar was a favorite of heaven and earth, the excellency of his country, and the happiest of men." Saner intellect than his never trod this earth, and could he speak to our age, with its fret and fever, his message would certainly include some words about the companionship of good books.

The supreme privilege of our generation is not rapid transit, nor the increase of comforts and luxuries. Modern civilization hath its flower and fruitage in books and culture for all through reading. Should the dream of the astronomer ever come true, and science establish a code of electric signals with the people of Mars, our first message would not be about engines, nor looms, nor steamships. Not the telephone by which men speak across continents, but the book by which living men and dead men converse across centuries, would be the burden of the first message. President Porter once said that the savage visiting London with Livingstone appreciated everything except the libraries. The poor black man understood the gallery, for the face of his child answered to that of Raphael's cherub and seraph. He understood the cathedral, with its aisles and arches, for it reminded him of his own altars and funeral hymns. He understood the city, for it seemed like many little towns brought together in one. But the great library, crowded from floor to ceiling with books, the strange, white pages over which bowed the reader, while smiles flitted across his face as one sun-spot chases another over the warm April hills, the black marks causing the reader's tears to flow down upon the open page, made up a mystery the poor savage could not understand. No explanation availed for the necromancy of the library.

For wise men the joys of reading are life's crowning pleasures. Books are our universities, where souls are the professors. Books are the looms that weave rapidly man's inner garments. Books are the levelers--not by lowering the great, but by lifting up the small. A book literally fulfills the story of the Wandering Jew, who sits down by our side and like a familiar friend tells us what he hath seen and heard through twenty centuries of traveling through Europe. Newton's "Principia" means that at last stars and suns have broken into voice. Agassiz's zoology causes each youth to be a veritable Noah, to whom it is given to behold all insects and beasts and birds going two by two into the world's great ark. God hath given us four inferior teachers, including travel, occupation, industry, conversation, and four teachers superior, including love, grief, death--but chiefly books.

Wisdom and knowledge are derived from sources many and various. Like ancient Thebes, the soul is a city having gates on every side. There is the eye gate, and through it pass friends, a multitude of strangers, the forests, the fields, the marching clouds. There is the ear gate, and therein go trooping all sweet songs, all conversation and eloquence, all laughter with Niobe's woe and grief. There is conversation, and thereby we cross the threshold of another's mind, and wander through the halls of memory and the chambers of imagination. But these faculties are limited. The ear was made for one sweet song, not for a thousand. Conversation is with one friend living, not with Pliny and Pericles. The vision stays upon yonder horizon; but beyond the line where earth and sky do meet are distant lands and historic scenes; beyond are battle-fields all stained with blood; beyond are the Parthenon and the pyramids. So books come in to increase the power of vision. Books cause the arctics and the tropics, the mountains and hills, all the generations with their woes and wars, their achievements for liberty and religion, to pass before the mind for instruction and delight. And when books have made men contemporaneous with Socrates and Cicero, with Emerson and Lowell, when they have made man a citizen of every clime and country, they go on to add advantages still more signal. When the royal messenger brought Newton the announcement of the honor bestowed upon him by the Queen, the astronomer was so busy with his studies relating to the "Principia" that he begrudged his visitor even an hour of his time.

The great man was too busy writing for thousands to talk long with a single individual about his discoveries of light and color and his proofs of the moon ever falling toward the earth. Not even to his best friends could the astronomer unfold through conversation what he gives us in his "Principia." When an American author called upon Carlyle he found him in a very peevish mood. Through two hours he listened to this student of heroes and heroism pour forth a savage tirade against all men and things. Never again was the American poet able to associate with Carlyle that fine poise, sanity, and reserve power that belong to the greatest. In his books Carlyle gives his friends, not the peevishness of an evening, but the best moods of all his life, winnowing his intellectual harvests.

Recently an author has given the world reminiscences called "Evenings" with Browning and Tennyson, with Bright and Gladstone. Yet an evening avails only for a few pleasantries, a few anecdotes, a few reminiscences. As well speak of spending an afternoon with Egypt or making an evening call upon Rome. Yet a volume of "In Memoriam" or "The Idylls of the King" enables one to overhear the richest and most masterly thoughts that occupied Tennyson through the best creative years in his career. So striking are the advantages books have over conversation that the brief biography of the Carpenter's Son makes us better acquainted with Jesus Christ than the citizens of Samaria or Bethlehem could possibly have been. To some Nicodemus it was given to hear Him discourse on the new heart; some lawyer heard His story of the good Samaritan; others midst the press and throng caught a part of the tale of the prodigal son. But the momentary glimpse, the fragmentary word, the rumors strange and contradictory, yielded only confusion and mental unrest. But this brief biography exhibits to us His entire career, sets each eager listener down beside Christ while He unrolls each glowing parable, each glorious precept, each call to inspiration and the higher life. Thus books acquaint us with the best men in their best moods.

Books have two advantages. Chiefly they are tools for the mind. The foot's step is short, but the engine lengthens the stride and hastens it. The smith's blow is weak, but the trip-hammer multiplies the might of man's hand. Thus books are mental machines, enabling the mind of man to reap in many harvest fields and multiply the mental treasures. It takes years for Humboldt to search out the wonders of the Andes Mountains and other years for Livingstone to thread his way through the jungles of Africa. But a book, during two or three evenings by the fireside, enables man to journey through the

Dark Continent without the dangers of fever, without experiencing the pain from the lion leaping out of the thicket to mutilate the arm of Livingstone. With a book we tramp over the mountains of two continents without once suffering the heavy fall over the precipice that weakened Humboldt. Books enable us to visit climes, cities, civilizations ancient and modern, that without them could never be seen during man's years, so few, and by man's strength, so insufficient. Great men and rich increase their influence by surrounding themselves by servants who fulfill their commands.

Each president and prime minister strengthens himself by a cabinet. But what if the peasant or workman could surround himself with a group of counselors and advisers that included a hundred of the greatest intellects of his generation? What if some Herschel should approach the youth to say, "You need your night's rest for sleep; but for you I will give the years for studying the stars and their movements?" What if some Dana should say, "For you I will decipher the handwriting upon the rocks, trace the movement of the ice plows, search out the influence of the flames as they turn rocks into soil for vineyards?" What if some Audubon should say, "For you I will go through all the forests to find out the life and history of the winged creatures, from the humming-bird to hawk and eagle?" What if Niebuhr should say, "For you I will decipher the monuments, all ruins and obelisks, all man's parchments and manuscripts for setting forth man's upward progress through the centuries?" But this is precisely what books do for us.

Saving man's time and strength, books also increase his manhood and multiply his brain forces. With them, a man of fourscore years ends his career wiser than, without them, he could have been, though he had lived and wrought through ten thousand summers and winters. This is what Emerson means when he says, "Give me a book, health and a June day, and I will make the pomp of kings ridiculous." When the Athenian youth, beloved of the gods, went forth upon his journey, one friend brought him a wondrous armor, proof against arrows; another brought a horse of marvelous swiftness; another brought a bow of great size and strength. Thus armed, the youth conquered his enemies. But when books have armed man against his foes, they go on to change his enemies into friends; they shield him against ignorance; they free him from superstition; they clothe him with gratitude. Thank God for books, cheering our solitude, soothing our sickness, refining our passions, out of defeat leading us to victory! That youth can scarcely fail of character, happiness and success who, day by day, goes to school to sages and seers; who by night hears Dante and Milton discourse upon Paradise; who has for his mentors in office and counting-room some Franklin or Solomon. Experience, supplemented by books, teaches youth more in one year than experience alone will teach him in twenty.

Books also preserve for us the spirit of earth's great ones, just as the cellar of the king holds wines growing more precious with the lapse of years. From time to time God sends to earth some man with a supreme gift called genius. Passing through our life and world, he sees wondrous sights not beholden of our eyes, hears melodies too fine for our dulled hearing. What other men behold as bits of coal, his genius transmutes into diamonds. In the darkness he sleeps to see some "Midsummer Night's Dream;" in the day he wakens to behold the tragedy or comedy in his friend's career. While he muses, the fires of inspiration burn within him. When the time comes, the inner forces burst out in book or song or poem, just as the tulip bulb when April comes publishes its heart of fire and gold. The book he writes is the choicest wine in life, "the gold made fine in the fires of his genius." Seldom come these elect ones, just as the bush burned only once during Moses' many years in the desert. Many foot hills must be united to produce one vast mountain. Only one range of Rockies is needed to support many states. One Mississippi also can drain a continent.

Thinking of these great ones, Milton said: "The book is the life-blood of the master spirit." Just as the wisdom spoken into the phonograph makes marks there to be reproduced at will, so books preserve and repeat the eloquence of the greatest. Through his "Excursion," when Wordsworth says, "I go to the fields to-day," the youth may whisper, "and I go with thee." He may also accompany Layard, going forth to study the old tablets and the monuments; with Scott he may ride with Ivanhoe to castle and tournament; with Virgil and Dante he may shiver at the brink of the inky river or exult over the first glimpse of Paradise.

Well did Charles Lamb suggest that men should say grace--not only over the Christmas festival, but also over the table spread with good books. For man has no truer friends, Earth offers no richer banquet. When Southey grew old and dim of vision, he was seen to totter into his library. Moving about from shelf to shelf the aged scholar laid his hand upon one favorite book and then upon another, while a rare sweet smile passed over his face, just as we lay hand tenderly upon the shoulder of some dear friend. Through their books his old friends, the heroes of the past, had told Southey of their innermost dreams, their passions, their aspirations, what braced them in hours of battle, how they endured when death robbed them of their best. Poor and lonely, full oft the poet had talked with these volumes as with familiar friends. So before he died Southey said to his books "Good night," ere in that bright beyond he said "Good morning" to their authors.

This divine injunction as to the companionship of books bids us search out the use and purpose of reading. Primarily, books are to be read for information and mental strength. The hunger of the body for bread and fruit is not more real than the hunger of the intellect for facts and principles. Knowledge stands in as vital relation to the growth of reason as iron and phosphate to the enrichment of the blood. Ignorance is weakness. Success is knowing how. Ours is a world in which the last fact conquers. In addition to his own experience and reflection, the young artist must stand in some gallery that brings together all the best masters. Standing beside the Elgin marbles in the British Museum, the sculptor must bathe and soak himself in the Greek ideal and spirit, until the Greek thought throbs in his brain, and he feels the Greek enthusiasm for strength in round, lithe arms, and limbs made ready for the race.

But in a large, deep sense, books are the galleries in which spirits are caught and fastened upon the pages. Books are storehouses into which facts and principles have been harvested. Just as a bit of coal tells us what ferns and flowers grew in the far-off era, so the book gives us the very quintessence of man's thoughts about life and duty and death. Nor is there any other way of gaining these vital knowledges. Life is too short to obtain them through conversation or travel. Nor is any youth ready for his task until he has traced the rise and growth of houses, tools, governments, schools, industries, religions. He must also compare race with race, land with land, and star with star. Asked about his ideas of the value of education, a man distinguished in railway circles answered: "I have learned that each new fact has its money value. Other things being equal, the judgment of the man who knows the most must always prevail." But books alone can supplement experience, and give the information that makes man ready against his day of battle.

It has been said, "For a thousand men who can speak, there is only one who can think; for a thousand men who can think, there is only one who can see." Since, then, the greatest thing in life is to have an open vision, we need to ask the authors to teach us how to see. Each Kingsley approaches a stone as a jeweler approaches a casket to unlock the hidden gems. Geikie causes the bit of hard coal to unroll the juicy bud, the thick odorous leaves, the pungent boughs, until the bit of carbon enlarges into the beauty of a tropic forest. That little book of Grant Allen's called "How Plants Grow" exhibits trees and shrubs as eating, drinking and marrying. We see certain date groves in Palestine, and other date groves in the desert a hundred miles away, and the pollen of the one carried upon the trade winds to the branches of the other. We see the tree with its strange system of water-works, pumping the sap up through pipes and mains; we see the chemical laboratory in the branches mixing flavor for the orange in one bough, mixing the juices of the pineapple in another; we behold the tree as a mother, making each infant acorn ready against the long winter, rolling it in swaths soft and warm as wool blankets, wrapping it around with garments impervious to the rain, and finally slipping the infant acorn into a sleeping bag, like those the Esquimos gave Dr. Kane.

At length we come to feel that the Greeks were not far wrong in thinking each tree had a Dryad in it, animating it, protecting it against destruction, dying when the tree withered. Some Faraday shows us that each drop of water is a sheath for electric forces sufficient to charge 800,000 Leyden jars, or drive an engine from Liverpool to London. Some Sir William Thomson tells us how hydrogen gas will chew up a large iron spike as a child's molars will chew off the end of a stick of candy. Thus each new book opens up some new and hitherto unexplored realm of nature. Thus books fulfill for us the legend of the wondrous glass that showed its owner all things distant and all things hidden. Through books our world becomes as "a bud from the bower of God's beauty; the sun as a spark from the light of His wisdom; the sky as a bubble on the sea of His Power." Therefore Mrs. Browning's words, "No child can be called fatherless who has God and his mother; no youth can be called friendless who has God and the companionship of good books."

Books also advantage us in that they exhibit the unity of progress, the solidarity of the race, and the continuity of history. Authors lead us back along the pathway of law, of liberty or religion, and set us down in front of the great man in whose brain the principle had its rise. As the discoverer leads us from the mouth of the Nile back to the headwaters of Nyanza, so books exhibit great ideas and institutions, as they move forward, ever widening and deepening, like some Nile feeding many civilizations. For all the reforms of to-day go back to some reform of yesterday. Man's art goes back to Athens and Thebes. Man's laws go back to Blackstone and Justinian. Man's reapers and plows go back to the savage scratching the ground with his forked stick, drawn by the wild bullock. The heroes of liberty march forward in a solid column. Lincoln grasps the hand of Washington. Washington received his weapons at the hands of Hampden and Cromwell. The great Puritans lock hands with Luther and Savonarola.

The unbroken procession brings us at length to Him whose Sermon on the Mount was the very charter of liberty. It puts us under a divine spell to perceive that we are all coworkers with the great men, and yet single threads in the warp and woof of civilization. And when books have related us to our own age, and related all the epochs to God, whose providence is the gulf stream of history, these teachers go on to stimulate us to new and greater achievements. Alone, man is an unlighted candle. The mind needs some book to kindle its faculties. Before Byron began to write he used to give half an hour to reading some favorite passage. The thought of some great writer never failed to kindle Byron into a creative glow, even as a match lights the kindlings upon the grate. In these burning, luminous moods Byron's mind did its best work. The true book stimulates the mind as no wine can ever quicken the blood. It is reading that brings us to our best, and rouses each faculty to its most vigorous life.

Remembering, then, that it is as dangerous to read the first book one chances upon as for a stranger in the city to make friends with the first person passing by, let us consider the selection and the friendship of books. Frederic Harrison tells us that there are now 2,000,000 volumes in the libraries, and that every few years the press issues enough new volumes to make a pyramid equal to St. Paul's Cathedral. Lamenting the number of books of poor quality now being published, this author questions whether or not the printing press may not be one of the scourges of mankind. He tells that he reads but few books, and those the great ones, and describes his shipwreck on the infinite sea of printer's ink, and his rescue as of one escaping by mercy from a region where there was water, water everywhere but not a drop to drink. Let us confess that books by their very multitude bewilder, and that careless and purposeless reading destroys the mind. Let us admit, too, that books no more mean culture than laws mean virtues.

Doubtless, individuality is threatened by the vast cataract of literature. As children, we trembled needlessly when the nurse told us that skies rained pitchforks, but as men we have a right to fear when the skies rain not pitchforks but pamphlets. Multitudes are in the condition of the schoolboy who, when asked what he was thinking about, answered that he had no thoughts, because he was so busy reading he had no time to think. Like that boy, multitudes to-day cannot see the wood for the trees. Many stand before the vast abyss of literature as Bunyan's pilgrim stood before the Slough of Despond, crying: "What shall I do?" The necessity of severe selection is upon us, but certain things all must read.

First of all, every year each young man and woman should take a fresh look about the world house in which all live. When Ivanhoe waked to find himself a prisoner in a strange castle he straightway explored the mansion, passing from chamber to banquet hall, and from tower to moat, and the high walls that shut him in. If, indeed, God did so dearly love this star as to use its very dust for making man in His own image, we ought to love and study well this world house, wherein is enacted the drama of man's life and death. Longfellow thought of our earth as a granite-sheathed ship sailing through air, with plate of mail bolted and clamped by the Almighty mechanism, the throbbings of Vesuvius hinting at the deep furnaces that help to drive her forward upon the voyage through space. But God's name for this earth house was Paradise. And a veritable paradise it is, with its vegetable carpet, soft and embroidered, beneath man's feet; with its valleys covered with corn until they laugh and sing; with its noble architecture of the mountains covered with mighty carvings and painted legends. Verily, it would be an ungracious thing for us to go on living here without taking the trouble to look upon this earth's floor, so firm and solid, or study the beauteous ceiling lighted with star lamps by night. And the evenings of one week with Geikie or Dana will tell us by what furnaces of fire the granite was melted, by what teeth of glaciers and weight of sea-waves the earth's surface was smoothed for the plow and the trowel. How long it has been since the glacier was a mile thick upon the very spot where we stand, how long since the waters of Lake Michigan, now flowing over Niagara, ceased flowing into the Mississippi.

The evenings of another week with Professor Gray or Grant Allen will tell us how all the trees and plants live and breathe and wax great; how the lily sucks whiteness out of the slough, and how the red rose untwists the sunbeam and pulls out the scarlet threads. The evenings of another week with Ball or Proctor or Langley will exhibit the sun pulling the harvests out of our planet, even as the blazing log pulls the juices out of the apples roasting before the hot coals; how large a house on the moon must be in order to be seen by the new telescope at Lake Geneva; whether or not the spots on the sun represent great chunks of unburned material, some of which are a full thousand miles across, materials thrown up by gaseous explosions. While Maury will take us during another week, in a glass boat that is water-tight, upon a long cruise more than three thousand leagues under the sea, showing us those graveyards called sea shells, those cities called coral reefs, those strange animals that have roots instead of feet, called sponges.

Having journeyed around the earth house, each should study himself; his body as an engine of mental thought, an instrument of conduct and character; the number and nature and uses of the forty and more faculties of mind and heart with which he is endowed. From the study of the soul the mind moves easily to the upward movement of the race, as man journeys from hut to house, from tent to temple, from force to self-government and education and literature, from his flaming altar to the rising hymn and aspiring prayer. This tells us what contribution each race, Hebrew and Greek, Roman and Teuton, has made to civilization. Then come the books of life, wherein the qualities to be emulated are capitalized in the lives of the great, for biography is one of man's best teachers. Therein we see how the hero bore up against his wrongs, his sorrows and defeats, and how he sustained himself in times of triumph. Phillips Brooks thought that the basis of every library should be biography, memoirs, portraits and letters. Nor should we forget the books of art, wherein the facts of life are idealized and carried up to beauty. Witness the dramas, poems, or the several great novels.

But apart from and above all others is the book, the Bible. Alone it has civilized whole nations. Be our theories of inspiration what they may, this book deals with the deepest things in man's heart and life. Ruskin and Carlyle tell us that they owe more to it in the way of refinement and culture than to all the other books, plus all the influence of colleges and universities. Therein the greatest geniuses of time tell us of the things they caught fresh from the skies, "the things that stormed upon them, and surged through their souls in mighty tides, entrancing them with matchless music"; things so precious for man's heart and conscience as to be endured and died for. It is the one book that can fully lead forth the richest and deepest and sweetest things in man's nature. Read all other books, philosophy, poetry, history, fiction; but if you would refine the judgment, fertilize the reason, wing the imagination, attain unto the finest womanhood or the sturdiest manhood, read this book, reverently and prayerfully, until its truths have dissolved like iron into the blood. Read, indeed, the hundred great books. If you have no time, make time and read. Read as toil the slaves in Golconda, casting away the rubbish and keeping the gems. Read to transmute facts into life, but read daily the book of conduct and character--the Bible. For the book Daniel Webster placed under his pillow when dying is the book all should carry in the hand while living.

THE SCIENCE OF LIVING WITH MEN

"There is an art of right living."--Arthur Helps.

"The supreme art life above all other arts is the art of living together justly and charitably. There is no other thing that is so taxing, requiring so much education, so much wisdom, so much practice, as the how to live with our fellow-men. In importance this art exceeds all productive industries which we teach our children. All skill and knowledge aside from that is as nothing. The business of life is to know how to get along with our fellow-men."--H.W. Beecher.

"As all the stars are pervaded by one law, in one law live and move and have their being, so all minds that reason and all hearts that beat, act in one empire of one king; and of that vast kingdom, the law the most sweeping, the most eternal, is the law of loving kindness."--Swing.

"The nations have turned their places of art treasure into battle-fields. Fancy what Europe would be now if the delicate statues and temples of the Greeks--if the broad and massive walls of the Romans, if the noble and pathetic architecture of the Middle Ages, had not been ground to dust by mere human rage. You talk of the scythe of time and the tooth of time; I tell you time is scytheless and toothless; it is we who gnaw like the worm, we who smite like the scythe. All these lost treasures of human intellect have been wholly destroyed by human industry of destruction; the marble would have stood its 2,000 years as well in the polished statue as in the Parian cliff; but we men have ground it to powder and mixed it with our own ashes."--Ruskin.

XII

THE SCIENCE OF LIVING WITH MEN

The great writers of all ages have held themselves well away from any formal discussion of the art of right living and the science of a skillful carriage of one's faculties. Government, war and eloquence have indeed received full scientific statement, and those arts called music and sculpture have obtained abundant literary treatment. But, for some reason, no philosopher has ever attempted a formal treatise teaching the youth how to carry his faculties so as to avoid injuring his fellows and secure for them peace, happiness and success. Nevertheless, the art of handling marble is nothing compared to the art of handling men. Skill in evoking melody from the harp is less than nothing compared to skill in allaying discords in the soul and calling out its noblest impulses, its most energetic forces.

Nor is there any science or any productive industry whatsoever that is at all comparable to the science of just, smooth and kindly living. For the business of life is not the use and control of winds and rivers; it is not the acquisition of skill in calling out the secret energies contained in the soil or concealed in the sky. The business of life is the mastery of the art of living smoothly and justly with one's fellows and the acquisition of skill in calling out the best qualities of those about us. Indeed, the home and the market do but furnish practice-ground for developing expertness in carrying one's faculties. Sir Arthur Helps first coined the expression, "the art of right living," and society can never be sufficiently grateful to this distinguished scholar for reminding us that when every other art has been secured, every other science achieved, there still remains for mastery the finest of all the fine arts, the science of a right carriage of one's faculties midst all the duties and relations of home and school, of store and street.

Searching out for some reason why scientists have discussed friendship, reform, or patriotism, but have passed by the science of right living, we shall find the adequate explanation in the fact that this is the largest subject that can possibly be handled. It concerns the right carriage of the whole man, the handling of the body, and the maintenance of perfect health; the control of the temperament, with its special talent or weakness; the use of reason, its development and culture; the control of judgment, with the correction of its aberrations; it involves such a mastery of the emotions as men have over winds and rivers; it concerns conscience and conversation, friendship and commerce, and all the elements affectional and social, civic and moral.

For man stands, as it were, in the center of many concentric circles. About himself, as a center, sweeps the home circle; his immediate neighborhood relations describe a wider circle; his business career describes one larger still; then come his relations to the community in general, while beyond the horizon is a circle of influence that includes the world at large. When the tiny spider standing at the center of its wide-stretching and intricate web, woven for destruction, chances to touch any thread of the web, immediately that thread vibrates to the uttermost extremity. And man stands at the center of a vast web of wide-reaching influence, woven not for blighting, but for blessing, and every one of these out-running lines, whether related to friends near by or to citizens afar off, thrills and vibrates with secret influences; and there is no creature in God's universe so taxed as man, having a thousand dangers to avoid, and fulfilling ten thousand duties. He who would adequately discuss the science of right living must propose a method that will enable man to carry his faculties midst all the conditions of poverty or riches, of sickness or health, of the friendship of men or their enmity.

Discerning the largeness of this theme, many question whether right living can be reduced to a science, and, if so, whether it ever can be acquired as an art. We know that there is a science of government, a science of wealth, a science of war, and mastery in each department seems possible. Moreover, long practice has lent men skill in the arts. Even Paganini was born under the necessity of obtaining excellence in his art through practice. Titian also was a tireless student in color, and Macaulay himself toiled hard over his alphabet. Printers tell us that practice expels stiffness from the fingers and makes type-setting an automatic process. Daniel Webster was counted the greatest orator of his time; but there never lived a man who drilled himself in solitude more scrupulously, and his excellence, he says, was the fruit of long study.

Henry Clay had a great reputation as a speaker; but when the youth had through years practiced extemporaneous speech in the cornfields of Kentucky, he went on to train himself in language, in thought, in posture, in gesture, until his hand could wield the scepter, or beckon in sweet persuasion, until his eye could look upon his enemies and pierce them, or beam upon his friends and call down upon them all the fruits of peace and success. Nor has there been one great artist, one great poet, one great inventor, one great merchant, nor one great man in any department of life whose supremacy does not, when examined, stand forth as the fruit of long study and careful training. Men are born with hands, but without skill for using them. Men are born with feet and faculties, but only by practice do their steps run swiftly along those beautiful pathways called literature or law or statesmanship. Man's success in mastering other sciences encourages within us the belief that it is possible for men to master the science of getting on smoothly and justly with their fellow men. In importance this knowledge exceeds every other knowledge whatsoever. To know what armor to put on against to-morrow's conflicts; how to attain the ends of commerce and ambition by using men as instruments; how to be used by men, and how to use men, not by injuring them, not by cheating them, not by marring or neglecting them; but how through men to advance both one's self and one's fellows--this is life's task. For skill in getting on with men is the test of perfect manhood.

No other knowledge is comparable to this. It is something to know how to sail a vast ship; it is important to understand the workings of a Corliss engine; man does well to aspire to the mastery of iron and wood, and the use of cotton and wool; most praiseworthy the ambition to master arguments and ideas; but it is a thousand times more important to understand men. To be able to analyze the underlying motives; to attain skill in rebuking the worst impulses in men, and skill in calling forth their best qualities; to distinguish between selfishness and sincerity; to allay strife and promote peace; to maintain equanimity midst all the swirl of passion; to meet those who storm with perfect calm; to meet scowling men with firm gentleness; to meet the harshness of pride with a modest bearing; to be self-sufficing midst all the upheaval and selfishness of life--this is to be a follower of Christ, and He is the only gentleman our world has ever seen. Oh, for some university for teaching the art of right living! Oh, for some college teaching the science of attaining the personal ends of life without marring one's ideals! For life has only one fine art--the art of getting along smoothly with ourselves and our fellows.

Let us confess that man easily masters every other art and science. His discoveries as to stars and stones and shrubs provoke ever fresh surprise. His inventions, who can number? He easily masters winds and rivers. He takes the sting out of the thunderbolt and makes it harmless. Afterward with electric lamps he illumines towns. With invisible sunbeams he paints instantaneous pictures of faces, palaces, mountains, and landscapes. With the dark X-rays he photographs the bone incased in flesh, the coins contained in the purse. With his magnet the scientist throws a rope around the cathode rays and drags them whithersoever he will. In the field the inventor uses an electric hoe to kill the germs of the thistle and deadly nightshade. Strange that he cannot invent an instrument for killing the germs of hatred and envy in his own heart! The gardener easily masters the art of cultivating roses and violets, but breaks down in trying to produce in himself those beauteous growths called love, truth, justice--flowers, these, that are rooted in heaven, but blossom here on earth.

An expert driver will hold the reins over six fiery steeds, or even eight, but he descends from his coach to find that his own passions are steeds of the sun that run away with him, bringing wreckage and ruin. Man has skill for turning poisons into medicines. He changes deadly acids into balms, but he has no skill for taking envy's poisons out of the tongue, or sheathing the keen sword of hatred. As to physical nature, man seems rapidly approaching the time when all the forces of land and sea and sky will yield themselves as willing and obedient servants to do his will. But, having made himself monarch in every other realm, man breaks down utterly in attempting the task of living peaceably with his friends and neighbors. Sublime in his integrity and strength, he is most pitiable in the way he wrecks his own happiness, and ruins the happiness of others. Pestilence in the city, tornado in the country, the fire in the forest--these are but feeble types of man as a destroyer. One science is as yet unmastered by man--the science of right living and the art of getting along smoothly with himself and his fellows.

To-day the new science explains the difficulty of right living, by the largeness of man's endowment. There are few failures in the animal or vegetable world. Instinct guides the beast, while the shrub attains its end by automatic processes. No vine was ever troubled to decide whether it should produce grapes or thorns. No fig tree ever had to go to school to learn how to avoid bearing thistles. The humming bird, flying from shrub to shrub, hears the inner voice called instinct. These instincts serve as guide books. The animal creation that moves through the air or water or the forests experiences but little difficulty in finding out the appointed pathway. But the problem of rose, lark or lion is very simple and easy, compared with the problem of man. If the oak must needs bear acorns, man is like a vine that can at will bring forth any one of a hundred fruits. He is like an animal that can at its option walk or fly, swim or run. The pathway opened before the brute world is narrow and its task therefore is very simple, while the vast number of pathways possible to man often embarrasses his judgment and sometimes works bewilderment.

After thousands of years man is still ignorant whether it is best for him to eat flesh or confine himself only to fruit; whether the juice of the grape is helpful or harmful; whether the finest culture comes from confining one's study to a single language, as did Socrates and Shakespeare, or through learning many languages, as did Cicero and Milton; whether a monarchy or democracy is better suited for securing the people's happiness and prosperity; whether the love of God in front is a motive sufficient to pull a man heavenward, or whether fear and fire kindled in the rear will not lend greater swiftness to his footsteps. It is wonderful how many problems yet remain to be solved.

Nor could it be otherwise. As things increase in size and complexity the difficulty of handling them increases. It is easy to manage a spinning-wheel, but difficult to handle a Jacquard loom having hundreds of delicate parts. It is easy to use a boy's whistle, but hard to master the pipe organ with keys rising bank upon bank. Out of an alphabet numbering six and twenty letters all the sciences and arts can be fashioned; but the alphabet of man's faculties numbers four and forty letters. Who shall measure the divine literatures possible to all these combinations of thought, feeling and aspiration?

The scientist tells us that all of the instruments and excellences distributed among the animals are united in man.

Man has the beaver's instinct for building, the bee's skill for hiving, the lion's stroke is less than man's trip-hammer, the deer's swift flight is slowness to man's electric speed, the eagle itself cannot outrun his flying speech. It is as if all the excellences of the whole animal creation were swept together and compacted in man's tiny body, with the addition of new gifts and faculties; but this concentration of all the gifts distributed to the animal world in man means that the dangers and difficulties that are distributed over all the rest of the animal creation will also be concentrated upon his single person. The increase of his treasure carries with it the increase of danger and difficulty. The vastness of his endowment opens up the possibilities of innumerable blunderings and stumblings and wanderings from the way. By so much, therefore, as he is above the bird and the beast, by that much does the task of carrying aright his faculties increase in magnitude.

Moreover, smooth living with men is difficult because of the continual conflict with evil. Integrity can never be good friends with iniquity, nor liberty with tyranny, nor purity and sweetness with filth and foulness. There is no skill by which John can ever live in peace with Herod. Paul, the author of the ode to love, was always at war with Nero, and at last had his head shorn off. William Tell could not get along smoothly with Gesler, the tyrant who robbed the Swiss of their rights. When doves learn to live peaceably with hawks, and lambs learn how to get along with wolves, good men and true will learn how to live in peace with vice and crime. Wickedness means warfare, not peace.

Deviltry cannot be overcome by diplomacy. Not embassies, but regiments, overcome intrenched oppression. Men of integrity and refinement can have but one attitude toward corruption, drunkenness, parasitism, gilded iniquity-- the attitude of uncompromising hostility. Languorous, emasculated manhood may silently endure great wrongs for the sake of peace and quiet; but robust manhood never. One of the dangers of our age and nation is a tendency to conciliate wrong and smooth over wickedness through a spurious sense of charity. Genius gilds vice, and wit and brilliancy transform evil into an angel of light. Only expel dullness and make evil artistic, and it is condoned; but vice attired in the garb of a queen is as truly vice as when clothed in rags and living in squalor. To become accustomed to evil, to garnish sin, to dim and deaden sensibility to what is right and beautiful, is to extirpate manhood and become a mere lump of flesh. No man has a right to be good friends with iniquity. In a wicked world the only people who are justified in peaceable living are the people in graveyards. In an age and land like ours only men of mush and moonshine can be friends with everybody.

In view of the crime, poverty and ignorance of our age, for a man to live so that his friends can truthfully write on his tombstone, "He never had an enemy," is for him to be eternally disgraced. Such a man should never be guilty of showing his face in heaven, for he will find that the angels, at least, are his enemies. Looking toward integrity, Christ came to bring peace. Looking toward iniquity, Christ came to bring the sword. Not until every wrong has been turned to right, not until every storm has been stilled into peace, not until the fatherhood of God and the brotherhood of man have been incarnated in institutions, will conflict cease and smooth living toward all men become an actuality.

Ambition and the clashing of interests also mitigate against smooth living. Perhaps no age has offered more powerful stimulants to ambition. The field is open to all, and the rewards are great. Therefore Emerson's phrase, "infinite aspiration and infinitesimal performance." Contentment is the exception, aspiration is universal. Indeed, the national temptation is ambition. An American merchant lives more in a year than an Oriental in eighty years; more in an hour than an Indian merchant in twenty-four. So powerful are the provocatives to thinking and planning that cerebral excitement is well-nigh continuous. Moving forward, the youth finds every pathway open and is told that every honor and position are possible achievements; the result is that the individual finds himself competing with all the rest of the nation. How fierce the strife! What intense rivalries! What battles between opponents! What conflicts in business!

In politics, coveting national honors, men spend months in laying out a campaign. A vast human mechanism is organized with ramifications extending through the nation. As in the olden times in the court of King Arthur, knights entered the tournament and some Lancelot clothed in steel armor rode forth to meet some Ivanhoe in mortal combat; so it is to-day when one plumed knight meets another in the political arena--one conquers, and one is killed, in that he suffers a broken heart.

In commerce the strife is not less fierce. Men literally stand over against each other like gunboats, carrying deadly missiles. If to-morrow conflict and strife should spring up in each garden--if the rose should strike its thorn into the honeysuckle; if the violet from its lowly sphere should fling mire upon the lily's whiteness; if the wheat should lift up its stalk to beat down the barley; if the robin should become jealous of the lark's sweet voice, and the oriole organize a campaign for exterminating the thrush, we should have a conflict in nature that would answer to the strife and warfare in society. The universality of the conflicts in society is indicated by the fact that England's national symbol is not a dove, but a lion; America's is an eagle, and other nations' are the leopard and the bear. In national wars, where men by years of toil have planted vineyards, reared orchards, builded houses and cities, they proceed to burn up the homes, destroy the granaries, cut down the vineyards and orchards; and these periodic public quarrels do but typify the equally destructive private feuds and troubles. Darwin thought that men have descended from animals, and some men have so literally descended. Some seem to have come through the wolf; some have the fox's cunning; some have the lion's cruelty, and some are as combative as bull-dogs. Now, it is not easy to maintain one's dignity when a little cur nips your heels behind, and a mastiff threatens you before. And some men seem to unite both elements; they run behind you and nip, they go before to bark and threaten. Under such circumstances it is not easy to live smoothly and charitably. It is easy to tame lions, but to tame men is not easy. It is easy to breast the current of rivers, but to stand against the full force of public opinion is hard. But midst all life's conflicts and clashings this task is upon us. We are to maintain peace, love our enemies, and ultimately master the art of right living with our fellows.

To all persons interested in the betterment of society comes the reflection that getting on with men is life's abiding aim and end. Schools can teach no other knowledge comparable to this. It is important to train the child in music, to drill him in public speech, to teach him how to handle the horse and dog, how to swim and ride, the use of tools and engines, the nature and production of wealth; but it is of far greater importance that youth should be given a knowledge of men, and become a skillful student of human nature; to learn how to read the face as an open book. If the jurist studies men and their motives to find out the truth; if the physician studies men for reasons of diagnosis; if the merchant studies thinking of his profit, and the politician thinking of preferment, the citizen must understand his fellows in the interest of securing their happiness and highest welfare. Incidentally, it is important that a man should be well groomed and well kept; should be educated and refined, just as it is proper that the pipes of an organ should be decorated on the outside.

Nevertheless, the test of an organ is the melody and harmony within. And the test of manhood is not outer polish, but inner skill in carrying his faculties. Man is only a rudimentary man when in those stages he blunders in all his meetings with his fellows, and cannot buy nor sell, vote nor converse, without harming, marring, depressing, discouraging his fellow men. In our age many books have been written similar to Lyman Abbott's volume called "The Study of Human Nature," and the time has fully come when each child should be made ready for life's battle beforehand, and taught how to armor himself against the tournament. When the schools have trained the child to the use of tools, given the tongue skill in speaking and the mind skill in thinking, it remains to teach him the study of men, the peculiarities of each of the five temperaments; the nature and number of the animal impulses; the use of the social and industrial impulses; the control of the acquisitive and the spiritual powers. For man's carriage of himself in the presence of fire and forest is the least of his duties. That which will tax him and distress, and perhaps destroy him, will be the carriage of his faculties midst all the clash and conflict, the din and battle of market and street. And midst all the strife, this is to be his ideal--to bear himself toward his enemies and toward his friends, after the pattern of Him who "makes His sun to shine upon the evil and the good, His rain to fall upon the just and the unjust."

The measure of manhood is the degree of skill attained in the art of carrying one's self so as to pour forth upon men all the inspirations of love and hope, and to evoke good even from the meanest and wickedest of mankind. Passing through life, the soul is to be a happiness producer and a joy distributer. Without conscious thought the violets pour forth perfume; without volition the magnet pulls the iron filings; with no purpose the candle pushes its beams of light into the darkness; and such is to be the weight of goodness in each man, that its mere presence will be felt. For the soul carries power to bless or blight; it can lift up its faculties for smiting, as an enemy lifts the hammer above the fragile vase or delicate marble; through speech man can fill all the sky with storms, or he can sweep all clouds from the horizon. The soul can take the sting out of man's anger, or it can stir up anger; it can allay strife or whet the keen edge of hatred. The thermometer is not so sensitive to heat, the barometer to weight, the photographer's plate to light, as is the soul to the ten thousand influences of its fellow men.

For majesty and beauty of subtle influence, nothing is comparable to the soul. Not the sun hanging upon the horizon has such power for flower and fruitage as has a full-orbed Christian heart, rich in all good influences, throbbing with kindness and sympathy, radiant as an angel. Great is man's skill in handling engines of force; marvelous man's control of winds and rivers; wondrous the mastery of engines and ideas. But man himself is greater than the tools he invents, and man stands forth clothed with power to control and influence his fellows, in that he can sweeten their bitterness, allay their conflicts, bear their burdens, surround them with the atmosphere of hope and sympathy. Just in proportion as men have capacity, talent and genius, are they to be guardians, teachers, and nurses for men, bearing themselves tenderly and sympathetically toward ignorance, poverty and weakness. All the majesty of the summer, all the glory of the storms, all the beauty of galleries, is as nothing compared to the majesty and beauty of a full-orbed and symmetrical manhood. Should there be in every village and city a conspiracy of a few persons toward this refinement and culture, this beauty and sweet Christian living, the presence of these Christ-formed persons would transform the community. One such harvestful nature carries power to civilize an entire city. We no more need to demonstrate the worth of the sane, sound, Christ-like character than we need to prove the value of the all-glorious summer, when it fills the earth with fragrance, the air with blossoms, and all the boughs with luscious fruit. Each Christian youth is to be a man-maker and man-mender. He is to help and not hurt men. This is to walk in love. This is to overcome evil with good. This is to be not a printed but a living gospel. This is to be a master of the art of right living and a teacher of the science of character building.

THE REVELATORS OF CHARACTER

"Some men move through life as a band of music moves down the street, flinging out pleasure on every side through the air, to every one far and near, that can listen."--Beecher.

"Truth tyrannizes over the unwilling members of the body. No man need be deceived who will study the changes of expression. When a man speaks the truth in the spirit of truth, his eye is as clear as the heavens. When he has base ends, and speaks falsely, the eye is muddy, and sometimes asquint."--Emerson.

THE REVELATORS OF CHARACTER

In ancient times personal property bore the owner's trademark. All flocks and herds fed together upon the common. That each might know his own, the herdsman slit the ears of his sheep, or branded his oxen with the hot iron. Afterward, as wealth increased, men extended the marks of ownership. The Emperor stamped his image into the silver coin. The Prince wrought his initial into the palace porch. The peasant moulded his name into the bricks of his cottage. One form of property was slaves. Athens had 80,000 free citizens and 400,000 bondmen. As these slaves were liable to run away, their owners branded them. Sometimes a circle was burned into the palm, or a cross upon the forehead; and often the owner's name was tattooed upon the slave's shoulder. One of the gifts of antiquity to our modern life is the use of the trademark. To-day manufacturers blow their initials in the glass; they mould the trademark in steel, and weave it in tapestries.

Lying in his dungeon, everything reminded Paul of these marks of ownership. His chains bore the Emperor's initials. The slaves that brought him food carried Nero's brand. The very bricks of his dungeon floor were stamped with the tyrant's name. But, moving out from these marks of servitude, his vision swept a wider horizon. He, too, was property. A freeman, indeed, was he, yet he was not his own. Mind and heart were stamped with God's image and superscription. No hot iron had mutilated him, but trouble had wrought refinement, and love divine had left its indelible stamp. Gone indeed the fresh, bright beauty that was his when he sat a boy at Gamaliel's feet! Since the day when the mob in Lystra had lifted stones upon him; since the time of his scourging at Philippi, he had carried the marks of martyrdom. Suffering had plowed deep furrows in his face. But honorable were all his scars. They bore witness to his conquest over ease and self-indulgence. Dear to him these marks--they bound him to his Master, the Lord Jesus. They filled him with high hopes, for the same marks that made him a bond slave to God and immortality freed him from earth and earthly things. Musing, in kingly mood, the scarred hero exclaimed: "Let not hunger nor cold, let not the scourge nor the tyrant's threat trouble me, for I bear about in my body the marks of the Lord Jesus."

Now, God hath ordained that, like Paul's, every human body shall register personal history, publishing a man's deeds, and proclaiming his allegiance to good or evil. The human face and form are clothed with dignity in that the fleshly pages of to-day show forth the soul's deeds of yesterday. Experience teaches us that occupation affects the body. Calloused hands betray the artisan. The grimy face proclaims the collier. He whose garments exhale sweet odors needs not tell us that he has lingered long in the fragrant garden. But the face and form are equally sensitive to the spirit's finer workings. Mental brightness makes facial illumination. Moral obliquity dulls and deadens the features. There never was a handsome idiot. There never can be a beautiful fool. But sweetness and wisdom will glorify the plainest face.

Physicians tell us that no intensity of disease avails for expelling dignity and majesty from a good man's countenance, nor can physical suffering destroy the sweetness and purity of a noble woman's. It is said that after his forty days in the mount Moses' face shone. All the great artists paint St. Cecilia with face uplifted, listening to celestial music, and all glowing with light, as though sunbeams falling from above had transfigured the face of the sweet singer. Those who beheld Daniel Webster during his delivery of his oration on the Pilgrim Fathers say that the statesman's face made them think of a transparent bronze statue brilliantly lighted from within, with the luminosity shining out through the countenance.

But the eyes are the soul's chiefest revelators. Tennyson spoke of King Arthur's eyes as "pools of purest love." As there is sediment in the bottom of a glass of impure water, so there is mud in the bottom of a bad man's eye. Thus, in strange ways, the body tells the story of the soul. Health hangs its signals out in rosy cheeks; disease and death foretell their story in the hectic flush, even as reddening autumn leaves foretell the winter's heavy frost; anxious lines upon the mother's face betray her secret burdens; the scholar's pallor is the revelation of his life, while the closely knitted forehead of the merchant interprets the vexing problems he must solve.

Thinking of the pathetic sadness of Lincoln's face, all seamed as it was and furrowed with care and anxiety, Secretary Stanton said that the President's face was a living page, upon which the full history of the nation's battles and victories was written. We are told that when the Waldenses could no longer bear the ghastly cruelty of the inquisitors, they fled to the mountain fastnesses. There, worn out by suffering, the brave leader was stricken by death. Coming forth from their hiding-places, the fugitives gathered around the hero's bier. Stooping, one lifted the hair from the forehead of the dead youth and said: "This boy's hair, grown thin and white through heroic toil, witnesseth his heroism. These, the marks of his fidelity." Thus, for those who have skill to read the writing, every great man's face is written all over with the literature of character. His body condenses his entire history, just as the Declaration of Independence is condensed into the limits of a tiny silver coin.

Calm majesty is in the face of Washington; pathetic patience and divine dignity in that of Lincoln; unyielding granite is in John Brown's face, though sympathy hath tempered hardness into softness; intellect is in Newton's; pure imagination is in Keats' and in Milton's; heroic substance is in the face of Cromwell and in that of Luther; pathetic sorrow is found in Dante's eyes; conscience and love shine in the face of F閺elon. Verily, the body is the soul's interpreter! Like Paul, each man bears about in his body the marks, either of ignorance and sin, of fear and remorse, or the marks of heroism and virtue, of love and integrity. To the gospel of the page let us add the gospel of the face.

But let none count it a strange thing that the soul within registers its experiences in the body without. God hates secrecy and loves openness. He hath ordained that nature and man shall publish their secret lives. Each seed and germ hath an instinctive tendency toward self-revelation. Every rosebud aches with a desire to unroll its petals and exhibit its scarlet secret. Not a single piece of coal but will whisper to the microscope the full story of that far-off scene when boughs and buds and odorous blossoms were pressed together in a single piece of shining crystal. The great stone slabs with the bird's track set into the rock picture forth for us the winged creatures of the olden time. When travelers through the Rocky Mountains behold the flaming advertisements written on the rocks, the reflection comes to all that nature also uses the rock pages for keeping her private memoranda of all those events connected with her history of fire and flood and glacier. When we speak of a scientific discovery, we mean that some keen-eyed thinker has come upon a page of nature's diary and copied it for his printer. The sea shells lying upon the crest of the high hills make one chapter in the story of that age when the ocean's waves broke against the peaks of the high mountains.

Journeying in his summer vacation into the region about Hudson Bay, the traveler brings back pieces of coal containing tropic growths. These carbon notebooks of nature tell us of a time when the regions of ice and snow were covered with tropical fruits and flowers, and suggest some accident that caused our earth to tip and assume a new angle toward the sun. Indeed, our earth bears about in the body the marks of its entire history, so that the scientist is able to tell with wondrous accuracy the events of a hundred thousand years ago. Already the Roentgen ray foretells the time when "nothing shall be covered that shall not be revealed, neither hid that shall not be known; when that which was done in secret shall be proclaimed from the housetops." Professor Babbage, the mathematician, has said that the atmosphere itself is becoming one vast phonograph upon whose sensitive cylinder shall be written all that man hath said, or woman whispered. Not a word of injustice spoken, not a cry of agony uttered, not an argument for liberty urged, but it is registered indelibly, so that with a higher mathematics and a keener sight and sense, the future scientist may trace each particle of air set in motion with as much precision as an astronomer traces the pathway of a moving star or a distant planet.

Recently the story has been told of a burglar who accidently discharged a magnesium light connected with a kodak on the shelf. The hour was midnight and everyone in the house was asleep. But the kodak was awake and at work. Frightened by the sudden light, the thief fled, leaving his spoil behind. But he also left his face. The next day in the court the kodak convicted him. Thus the new science is causing each man to stand in the center of an awful photographic and telegraphic system which makes an indelible record of man's words and deeds. No breath is so faint that it can escape recording itself; no whisper so low, no plan so secret, no deed of evil so dark and silent. Memory may forget--but nature never. Upon the pages of the physical universe the story of every human life is perpetually before the judge of all the earth.

It is deeply interesting to see how each living thing bears about in its body the story of its degradation, or the history of its rise and exaltation. Even in things that creep and crawl, the whole life-history is swept together in the animal body. The ship barnacle began its career with two splendid eyes. But it used its vision to find an easy place upon the side of pier or ship. Giving up locomotion, it grew sleek and fat, and finally its big eyes grew dull through misuse, and now they are dead. When the squirrels left the forests in the west and journeyed out upon the open prairies, they began to burrow in the ground. Finally, for want of use, they lost all power of climbing. Among the birds the lazy cuckoo began by stealing the nest another bird had built. But it paid a grievous price for its theft, for now when the cuckoo is confined by man and wants a nest of its own it toils aimlessly, and has lost all power to make for itself a soft, warm nesting-place.

In northern climes the mistletoe has a healthy normal taproot. But in our rich soil it became too dainty for dirt, and chose the life of a parasite. So the little seed struck its outer roots into the bark of the oak, and lazily sucked away the tree's rich sap. Soon luxury and living upon another's life ruined the mistletoe, just as the generation of young Romans was ruined by the father's wealth; just as an active and healthy boy is wrecked when he begins to be a sluggard and goes to the aunt--some rich aunt--and waits for her to die. And since all the lower creatures bear about in the body the marks of the full life-history, it seems natural to expect that man's body, through its health and beauty, or weakness and decay, should tell the story of how the soul within has lived and wrought. A short journey through our streets will prove to us that iniquity sets its mark in the face. Dickens describes Fagin as a man who was solid bestiality and villainy done up in bone and tissue. Each feature was as eloquent of rascality as an ape's of idiocy. Contrariwise, in the kingdom of morals there are men who seem solid goodness, kindness, and virtue, bound together with fleshly bands. Even distant ancestors leave their marks in man's body.

It has recently been discovered that the handwriting of one of our presidents was almost exactly that in his grandfather's will. The Bourbon family has always been distinguished by the aquiline nose. One of the oldest New England families is known for its singular length and strength of arm. Beauty is a mark in one family, and size is a mark in the other. Because man is made in the image of God we naturally look for those divine trademarks in man's body called comeliness and complexion, just as we look for the artist's name on the corner of his picture, or the sculptor's name on the pedestal of his statue. By so much as a babe's cheek is higher than the blushing peach, it ought to be more beautiful. And because the trees of the forest go forward toward October and death arrayed in their brightest robes, we have a right to expect that man in his old age also will reach the highest beauty and perfection.

But not so. Man's history has been a history of selfishness and sin, and his body bears the marks thereof. His features are "seamed by sickness, dimmed by sensuality, convulsed by passion, pinched by poverty, shadowed by sorrow, branded by remorse." Men's bodies are consumed by sloth, broken down by labor, tortured by disease, dishonored by foul uses, until beholding the "marks" of character in the natural face in a glass multitudes would fain forget what manner of men they are. For the human face is a canvas, and nature's writing goes ever on. But as the wrong act or foul deed sets its seal of distortion on the features, so the right act or true thought sets its stamp of beauty. There is no cosmetic for homely folks like character. Even the plainest face becomes beautiful in noble and radiant moods. He who ever beholds the vision of Christ's face will at last so take on the likeness of his Master as to bear about in his body also "the marks of the Lord Jesus."

Consider the habits and the unconscious desires as marks of character. When Arnold of Rugby took his boys for a holiday to London he found the revelators of personality in the objects which they first visited. The youth who had spent each spare moment in sketching made his way immediately to the gallery. Young Stanley, even then brooding upon moral themes, turned his face toward the abbey, whose fame he was to augment. The eager aspirant for political honors rushed toward the houses of Parliament. Thus also the students of physiognomy try to catch the subject off his guard, when the unconscious and habitual lines appear in the face. The kind of books one loves to read, the amusements one seeks, the friends he chooses, are all revelators. Recently an English traveler published a volume of impressions concerning America. Finding little to praise, the traveler finds much to criticise and blame. During his two or three weeks' sojourn in our cities, he tells us that he found sights and scenes that would shame Sodom and Gomorrah, and bemoans the fact that in this young, fresh land things should be as bad as in London and Paris, whither the scum and wrecks of society have drifted.

What a revelation! not of the city, but of the critic himself. But because he was interested in other things, the editor of an English Review found here material for a fruitful discussion of "The Higher Life of American Cities." Multitudes have sojourned here during a score of years and have not so much as heard of orgies and excesses. Yet if the bee is blind to all save flowers; if the worm cares only for rotten wood; if the mole bores downward, so there are natures that cannot rest until they have ferreted out that which they lovingly seek and eagerly desire to find. Habits also reveal personality. First the river digs the channel, then the channel controls the river, and when the faculties, by repetition, have formed habits, those habits become grooves and channels for controlling the faculties. What grievous marks were in poor Coleridge! Once this scholar spent a fortnight upon an annual address. But while the audience was assembling Coleridge left his friends and stepped out the rear door of the hall to go in search of his favorite drug, leaving his audience to master its disappointment as best it could.

And here is Robert Burns, bearing about in his body also the marks of his ownership. For this matchless genius was wrecked and ruined not by the wiles of him of the cloven foot, but by temptations that have been called "godlike." This glorious youth was not beguiled from the path by a desire to be a cold and calculating villain in his treatment of Jean, or to die of drink in his prime, or to leave his widow and orphans in poverty. Burns loved upward, loved noble things and beautiful; and his very love of beauty and grace, his love of good company, of wit, laughter and song, and all the stormy splendors of youth at springtide--these are the snares and wiles that caught his beautiful genius and led it away captive.

To-day, for him who hath eyes to see, the marks of a like immoderation are upon our generation also. What a revelation of the taste of our age is found in the new love of highly spiced literature! All history holds no nobler literature than that in the English tongue. Our poetry furnishes nectar for angels! Our philosophies bread for giants! The essayists furnish food for the gods! Nevertheless, a multitude have turned from this glorious feast to the highly spiced literature of fiction.

A traveler tells of watching bees linger so long beside the vats of the distillery that they became maudlin. And the love of high stimulants in literature is one of the character marks of our generation. Excess threatens our people. Men are anxious to be scholars and hurry along a pathway that leads straight to the grave. Men are anxious to find pleasure, but they find the flowers were grown in the church-yard. Men are feverishly anxious for wealth, and, coining all time and strength into gold, they find they have no health with which to enjoy the gathered sweetness. Haste in cooking the dinner has destroyed the appetite. We are told that "moderation and poise are the secrets of all successful art," as they are of all successful life. Give the rein to appetite and passion, and satiety, disenchantment, and the grave quickly come. Health, happiness, and character are through restraint. Thus truly, habit and trait in the individual or the generation become a mark in the body that is the revelator of character.

What men call character to-day is really another one of the marks of the Lord Jesus. Now and then a man appears in society from whose very presence there emanates an atmosphere and a sense of power--power that seizes upon the imagination of the beholder and holds him breathless, even as one stands breathless when overtaken by some sense in nature of overmastering sublimity. These strangely gifted men have appeared only at intervals of centuries. If an ordinary man is attacked in a lonely spot by armed footpads, he finds himself helpless. But history tells of a man who carried such reserves that, bound and unaided, he could deliver himself from an entire band of robbers. Surprised one day by a company of bandits, he was knocked down, robbed, and bound. But when he recovered consciousness, he argued the ropes off his wrists, talked his purse and rings out of the robbers' pockets back into his, bound his enemies--not with cords, but with linked words--led them back to the city instead of away from it, and landed the waylayers in jail.

Similarly, history tells us of half a score of men during the past two thousand years who have carried this same all-commanding atmosphere. For over a century students of oratory have been endeavoring to explain the eloquence of Whitefield. Such power had this man that the statesmen and philosophers of London used to leave the metropolis on Saturday and journey far into the country to join the crowds, often numbering twenty thousand people, that followed this preacher from village to village. David Hume, the skeptic, explained Whitefield's charm by saying that the preacher spake to his audience with the same passionate abandon with which an ardent lover speaks to his sweetheart when he pleads for her hand. But Benjamin Franklin tells us that the charm in Whitefield's speech was not his musical voice, not his stream of thought running clear as crystal, not his sudden electric outbursts, when the great man seemed on fire; the something that men have tried in vain to analyze, was his character--goodness and sincerity glowing and throbbing in and through words, just as the electric current glows and throbs through the connecting wires. Another such man, but lesser, was Lamartine. During the French Revolution, when the mob poured through the streets, sweeping before it the soldiers who opposed its progress, Lamartine made his way to the middle of the street and stood before the brutal leaders. So powerful was the influence of the good man's character, that, when the leader said, "Soldiers, we are in the presence of a man who represents seventy years of noble living," the rude mob uncovered. Afterward, when the insurgents laid down their arms, it was as a tribute to the superiority of character to guns and brute force.

But when we read of these all-commanding natures, we are not to think that these inspirational beings had their influence through some strange magnetic power, nor that they cast a spell over people like unto the spell that the cat casts over the mouse with which it plays. Their might has, for the most part, been the might of goodness. The chief mark that Paul and Wesley and Wilberforce, and all the great have carried about in the body has been the mark of character. What beauty is to the statue; what ripeness is to the fruit; what strength is to the body; what wisdom is to the reason--that character is to the soul!

Great is the power of bonds and gold! Mighty the influence of customs and institutions! But the greatest force that can exist in society is the presence and power of good men. As rain and soil and sunbeams are only raw materials, to be brought together and condensed into the ripe fruit, so tools, knowledge, goods, are but raw materials, to be wrought up into the fine substance of character. Happy all who have subordinated the animal impulses and the industrial faculties to the moral sentiments. Thrice happy they who have carried all their faculties up unto harmony and symmetry. All such, like Paul, bear about in the body the marks of the Lord Jesus.

MAKING THE MOST OF ONE'S SELF

"Till we all come unto the perfect man."--St. Paul.

"Every soul is a seed. It does not yet appear what it shall be."--H.

"'Very early,' said Margaret Fuller, 'I perceived that the object of life is to grow.' She herself was a remarkable instance of the power of the human being to go forward and upward. Of her it might be said, as G 鯨 the said of Schiller: 'If I did not see him for a fortnight, I was astonished to find what progress he had made in the interim.'"--James Freeman Clarke.

"Persons who are to transform the world must be themselves transformed. Life must be full of inspiration. If education is valuable, the age must double it; if art is sweet and high, we must double its richness and might; if philanthropy is divine, we must double its quantity and tenderness; if religion is valuable, double its truths and hasten with it unto more firesides; if man's life is great, let him count more precious all its summers and winters. The one duty of life is, lessen every vice and enlarge every virtue."--David Swing.

XIV

MAKING THE MOST OF ONE'S SELF

Two great principles run through all society. First comes the principle of self-care and self-love. Each man is given charge of his own body and life. By foresight he is to guard against danger. By self-defense he is to ward off attack. By fulfilling the instincts for food, for work and rest he is to maintain the integrity of his being. Upon each individual rests the solemn obligation to make the most possible of himself, and to store up resources of knowledge and virtue, of friendship and heart treasure. But when a man has treated his reason as a granary and stored it with food, his memory as a gallery, and filled it with pictures of a beautiful past, his reason and will as armories, and stored them with weapons against the day of battle, then a second principle asserts itself. Responsible for his own growth and happiness, man is made equally responsible for the happiness and welfare of those about him. By so much as he has secured his own personal enrichment, by that much he is bound to secure the enrichment and social advantage of his fellows. To love one's self at the expense of one's fellows is for selfness to become malignancy. To love one's neighbors more than one's self is foolishness and self-destruction.

Whatever of value the individual has, comes from fidelity to the first of these principles. Self-love working toward reason makes a man a scholar; working toward his imagination, makes him artist and inventor; working toward his gift of speech, makes him an orator; working with pride makes him self-reliant and self-sufficing. And when the principle of love for others asserts itself, this love, working toward poverty, transforms man into a philanthropist; working toward iniquity, makes man a reformer; working toward freedom, makes him a patriot and a hero; working toward God, makes him a saint and a seer.

The new astronomy makes much of the three cosmic laws. Our earth, by a form of self-love called molecular attraction, ceases to be scattered dust, and takes on the shape of a rich and beautiful planet. But self-loved, our earth is also sun-loved, and drawn by invisible bands it is swept forward out of winter into summer. Then enters in a third principle, by which Neptune and Uranus, lying upon the edge of space, seek fellowship with our planet and hold it at a fixed distance from the sun's fierce heat. Thus self-love has given the earth individuality, the love of other planets secures stability, while the sun's love gives movement and wealth. Working together, these three principles secure the harmony and stability of the planetary world. Similarly, each individual is part of a great social system. Each moves forward under the embrace of three laws, called love to God, love to neighbor, and love to self. Upon obedience to these laws rests all social wealth and civilization.

We hear little of individualism, and much of the solidarity of society. A bloodless and selfish destruction of the rights of the many has threatened the very foundations of human happiness and compelled the recognition of the fact that the weakness and injury of one are the weakness and injury of all. Ours is a world in which the law of the survival of the fittest not only works, but works very rapidly. Thus the more wealth a man has the more he can achieve. To-day, it is said, the various members of the Rothschild family in the different capitals of Europe control nine billions of dollars. This sum is accumulating like a rolling snowball, and will soon surpass, and perhaps absorb the wealth of several of the smaller European nations. Similarly, in the realm of wisdom, the more a man knows the more he can know. Sir William Jones tells us that he gave five years to mastering his first language, while six weeks were sufficient for acquiring his fortieth dialect. Thus, too, in the realm of inventive skill, each tool becomes the parent of a score of other tools. The studies preparatory to Edison's first mechanism covered a long period of years; but, gaining momentum, his inventive skill increased in geometric ratio, until to-day the famous electrician holds nearly a thousand patents; but, as nothing succeeds like success, so nothing is so ruinous as failure. The weaker a man is, the weaker he must become. When a man who seeks employment is shabby and gaunt and nerveless, his poverty lessens his chances, but tomorrow he will be weaker and shabbier, and day by day the rapidity of his declension will increase.

Startled by these considerations, our generation perceives that success feeding upon its gains will soon drink up all the energies of the earth, while failure, growing more ruinous, will sweep multitudes into the abyss. Therefore, society has come to fully recognize the importance of a mutual love and mutual service. When a man falls we are less and less ready to kick him. If the poorly born drops behind in life's race, society is increasingly ready to set him upon some beast. If some man's brain is spongy, and his mental processes slow, the stronger minds are belting his faculties to their swifter energies. If a man's moral springtime is slow, says one of our social reformers, society fits up for him a little ethical conservatory, with steam heat and southern exposure, where the buds are given a little judicious stimulating and pushing.

Society is recognizing the debt of strength to weakness. The man who has skill in speech is becoming a voice for the dumb. Those who have skill toward wealth are becoming the almoners of bounty toward art, education and morals. Men who selfishly get much and give little, who have become Dead Seas of accumulated treasure, are losing their standing in society. More and more cities are bestowing their honors and esteem upon those who serve their fellows. Men are becoming magazines, sending out kindness everywhither. Men are becoming gardens, filling all the air with pungent fragrance. Men are becoming castles, in which the poor find protection. The floods of iniquity have long covered the earth, but love is the dove bringing the olive branch of peace. Love sings the dawn of a new day.

Our generation does well to emphasize the principle of social sympathy and social liability. But, because individual worth is being threatened, the time seems to have fully come for also emphasizing man's duty to love and make the most of himself. Of late, self-care and self-enrichment, as a principle of life, have been berated and harshly condemned. Yet Christ recognized selfness as a principle most proper and praiseworthy and one to be used as the basis and measure of all moral worth. By so much as man loves and secures for himself the physical benefits and social incitements of life, by that much he is to love his fellows. And the failure to love one's self wisely and passionately ends by making it impossible for man to love his fellows. Plato's thought is ever with us: "The granary must be filled before the poor are fed; knowledge must be gained before knowledge is given." Happy the philanthropist whose generosity has founded school or library. But this gift of to-day is made possible only by the industry and thrift of yesterday. Happy the surgeon whose skill in a crisis hour has saved some valuable life. But the hand that performs what seems a miracle of surgery has back of it twenty years of vigilant study and practice.

Ours is a world in which the amount of wisdom or wealth or friendship to be distributed is predetermined by the amount required. The flow of the faucet is determined by the fullness of the reservoir. The speed of the electric car is fixed by the energy stored in the power house. The power of the piston is in the push of the accumulated steam. The Nile has force to feed civilizations, because there are a thousand streams and rivers, a thousand hills and mountains lying back of the Nile's current, and crowding it forward. If we could sit down by the famous Santa Barbara vine, and speaking with it as with a familiar friend, ask how it came to give man a half-ton of purple treasure in a single summer, the reply would be that this rich treasure was grown and given in one summer because two hundred summers were given to growing a vast root and trunk, to large stems and stalks.

When Nestor stood forth before the Greek generals and counseled attack upon Troy, he said: "The secret of victory is in getting a good ready." Wendell Phillips was once asked how he acquired his skill in the oratory of the lost arts. The answer was: "By getting a hundred nights of delivery back of me." Shakespeare tells us all that the clouds give in rain what they get in mist, which is the poet's way of saying that what he gave in inspiration he got by way of perspiration. Some years ago a young man asked a distinguished scholar and writer what he thought of the higher education. "If I were twenty, and had but ten years to live," answered the publicist, "I would spend the first nine years accumulating knowledge and getting ready for the tenth." Indeed, the measure of influence in any man is the measure of his reserves. The youth who will rule to-morrow is the youth who to-day is storing up resources of knowledge and wisdom, of self-reliance and courage.

All history does but repeat the principle. Surveying the past, we note that the nations that have made great contributions to civilization have been isolated. Our historians tell us that the Hebrew gave conscience and morals, the Greek reason and culture, the Roman law and government, the Teuton liberty and the rise of woman. But, singularly enough, not one of these nations lived in an open, extended country. Each forceful race has dwelt upon some island or peninsula. The Hebrew was shut in between the desert and the sea, and there restrained until he accumulated his moral treasure. He was compelled to fall back upon his own resources. By practice he found out that it was not best to steal; that society lived more happily and peacefully when the property of each individual was respected. Similarly, God gave him the work of formulating each of the ten commandments. Slowly the moral treasure grew. The jurist gave law, the poet sang songs, the prophet poured out his rhapsody, the patriot and martyr died for principle, and the roll of the heroes lengthened. At last the pages of Jewish history were filled with names glowing and glorious as the nights with stars.

Then came Jesus Christ, filling all the land with spiritual energies. Soon the pressure of moral forces was so strong as to break through all restraints. Then these moral treasures poured forth over all the earth. Having given the two thousand years before Christ to accumulating its moral energies, the Hebrew race acquired momentum enough to continue the civilizing tide through the two thousand years after Christ. Similarly Greece, the mother of the arts and sciences, was shut in between the mountains and the sea until the intellectual tides grew deep and strong.

But not alone does history urge us to make the most of ourselves. All our great men illustrate the same principle. Of late attention has been called to the fact that our cities are being ruled by men whose childhood and youth were spent in the country. Isolated, brooding for years in the fields and forests, these boys developed a forceful individuality. A recent canvass of the prominent men in New York City showed that eighty-five per cent were reared in the villages and rural districts. Seventeen of our twenty-three presidents came from the farm. A census of the colleges and seminaries in and about Chicago showed that the country is furnishing eighty per cent of our college students. The chances of success seem one hundred to one in favor of the country boy. Many explain this by saying that there is a mathematical relation between a fine physique and a firm, intellectual tread. Good thinking rests upon fine brain-fiber. But this is only half the truth.

These giants from the country learned in youth not to depend upon books and newspapers, but upon their eyes and ears. Having no external resources, they turned their thoughts inward and led forth their own faculties. They did not wait until they opened the journal to find out what they thought about some important subject, but, unaided, they wrought out their own opinions, and through self-reliance grew great. Should any sower go forth to sow in the streets of the city, he would reap but a small harvest. The hard, beaten roadway would give the grain no lodgment; but sown on the open furrows, the seed roots and grows. Thus the mind of the city youth is a roadway beaten down by the myriad events of life. His individuality is a root having little chance to grow.

The mornings rain newspapers, the evenings increase events, the very skies rain pamphlets. Individuality is overwhelmed with many things. Soon the mind ceases to develop its own mental treasure, and is content to receive its incitements from without. Because schools and colleges are multiplied, the youth who has never gone to the bottom of a single subject imagines that he is a fine student. Because his shelves are crowded with books, the man deceives himself into thinking that he has read them all. Because our age is rich in mechanical appliances and inventions, many who cannot drive a nail straight imagine that they have been really instrumental in ushering in this magnificent epoch. Many sing peans of exultation over this wondrous civilization who are mental and industrial paupers, whose chief ground of congratulation is that they got themselves born into this particular century. But power does not come that way. Moses will control all our jurists to-morrow because he spent forty years in the desert reflecting upon the principles of justice. Paul had the honor to fashion our political institutions because he gave twelve years of general preparation and three years of special application to the study of individual rights. Milton tells us that he spent four and thirty years of solitary and unceasing study in accumulating his material for a heroic poem that the world would not willingly let die.

Homer wrote the "Iliad" because he was blind and driven in upon his own resources. Dante wrote his "Inferno" because he was exiled, and in isolation had time to store up his mental treasure. Webster and Lincoln spent years in the forests and fields, reflecting and brooding, analyzing and comparing. Many a long summer passed while they sowed and garnered their mental treasure. Pasteur gave our generation much, because for thirty years he isolated himself and got much to give. When Lowell speaks of the attar of roses, he reminds us of the whole fields of crimson blossoms that have been swept together in one tiny vial. When Starr King saw the great trees of California standing forth twenty-five feet in diameter and lifting their crowns three hundred feet into the sunshine, he was so impressed by their dignity and beauty as to be touched into tears; but the size of the trees did not explain his emotion. It was the thought of the reserve energies that had been compacted into them. The mountains had given their iron and rich stimulants, the hills had given their soil, the clouds had given their rain and snow, a thousand summers and winters had poured forth their treasure about the vast roots. Thus the authors and statesmen who will help the next generation are to-day engaged in loving themselves and making the most of their talents. Not until they have compacted within themselves a thousand knowledges and virtues will they be able to love others.

With sadness let us confess that our age is sinning grievously against this principle of self-care and self-love. Individual worth is being sorely neglected. An age is great not through a large census roll, but through a multitude of great souls, just as a book is valuable not by having many pages, but by containing great ideas. The paving-stones in our streets are very different from sapphires. The bringing together of 65,000,000 small granite blocks will not turn these stones into diamonds. It is only when each stone is a gem that the increase of number means the increase of beauty. No nation is moving forward toward supremacy merely because the weak individuals began to go in droves. In our education we are singing peans and praise about our schools and new methods of education. Meanwhile Frederic Harrison insists that in fifty years the public schools of Great Britain have turned out not one mind of the first order. Some of those who have achieved renown in literature or statecraft were self-educated. The rest enjoyed the help of some parent or friend, who very early in the child's career took the pains to search out the child's strongest faculty, and then asked some tutor or teacher to assist in nourishing the special talent toward greatness.

At home, President White is telling us that our authors and poets are dead, and have no successors. Nor could it be otherwise. When a skillful driver wishes to develop the speed of a thoroughbred colt, he specializes upon this one animal. No sensible horseman would put forty colts upon a track and try to develop their speed by driving them around in a drove. It remains for the parents of this country to adopt the method of training their children in droves, and educating them in herds. Our common-school system began in the necessity for the division of labor. Settling in the wilds of New England, the men went into the forests with axes, or to the field with their hoes. The mothers went into the garden or to the loom. Rather than that their children should have no education, many parents came together and asked some one man or woman to do the work for all. Thus our common schools were born out of poverty and emergency.

But at length has come a time when parents, in blind worship of a system, have farmed their children out to intellectual wet-nurses. Many children who possess talent of the first order in the realm of poetry or literature are compelled during the most precious period of life to spend years upon subjects that yield them no culture effect. Meanwhile their enthusiasm is wasted, and their strongest faculties starved. Only when it is too late do they discover the cruel injustice that has been wrought upon them, and recognize that they must remain unfulfilled prophecies. Our common schools have wrought most effectively for our civilization. They are the hope of society. But not until our parents become enthusiastic teachers, and our homes assist the school rooms, will men cease complaining that the nation's great men have no successors, and that genius has departed from our people.

The time has fully come for the nation also to begin to love itself. All perceive that the individual has no right to be so generous to-day as to have nothing to bestow to-morrow. Wisdom guards to-day's expenditures lest to-morrow's capital be impaired. He is a poor husbandman who so overtaxes his fields or vineyards as to exhaust the soil or destroy the vine. Yet many events seem to prove that our nation has sorely injured itself by over-kindness. It has forgotten that only God can love everybody. In trying to help the many it has threatened its power to help any. It has been like a man who on a January day opens his windows and tries to warm all out of doors, only to find that he has frozen his family within the house, and warmed no one without. If we journey into the factory towns in New England, where the youthful Whittier and Longfellow were trained, we find the school-houses with windows boarded over. The little churches also are deserted and the doors nailed up. Listening to the "reformers" in our parks on a Sunday afternoon, we are amazed by the virulent attacks upon our institutions. Conversing with the foreman of a large group of men laying water-pipes, we are astonished at his statement that he has not a single man who can write well enough to keep the time and hours of these toilers. Standing in Castle Garden, where the emigrant ship unloads its multitudes, we hear the physician exclaim: "It will take this nation a hundred years to expel this vice and scrofula from its blood."

As some railways water their stock, and for each dollar issue bonds for five, in the hope that only one of the five will ever know enough to ask for their dollar, so the intelligence of the nation has been watered and diluted. Sometimes a whole ballot-box full of voters' tickets does not contain the common sense of a single vote of the days of Hamilton. Our nation often seems like a householder who has given his night-key to an enemy who has threatened his home with firebrands. Our nation has loved--not wisely, but too well. The time has come when it must choose between loving itself and becoming bankrupt in intelligence and morality. For purposes of educating the nations of the world as to the true value of free institutions, one little New England community, where all the citizens were patriots and heroes, scholars and Christians, where vulgarity and crime were unknown, where the jail was empty and the church was full, where all young lives moved toward the school-house--one such community has a value beyond our present millions.

What the world needs is not multitudes, but examples and ideals. If one Plato can be produced, he will lift the world. Our citizens ask artists to paint their pictures--not bootblacks. We ask architects to erect our public buildings--not chimney sweeps. Loving their city, our citizens have lined the avenues with beautiful homes and streets with stores and factories. But here their self-love stops. When great men have created the city, they ask saloon-keepers to govern it. Well did the sage say, it was as if we had passed by Daniel Webster and asked an African ape to speak in his stead. Strange--passing strange--that our nation and city should forget that all love for others begins with a wise love for self.

We return from our survey with the conviction that Jesus Christ did well to make individual worth the genius of Christianity. Having moved backward along the pathway of history, we have found the streams of civilization taking rise in some one enriched mind and heart, even as mighty rivers issue from isolated springs. Looking backward we see Moses building the Hebrew temple; we see Pericles and Plato fashioning many shapes of truth and beauty for Athens; we see Dante laying the foundations of Florence; we see Carlo Zeno causing Venice to rise out of the sands of the sea; we see Bacon and Luther rearing the cathedrals of thought and worship, under which the millions find their shelter. Oppressed by a sense of human ignorance and human sin, a thousand questions arise. Can one poorly born journey toward greatness of stature? The Cremona violin of the sixteenth century is a mass of condensed melody. Each atom was soaked in a thousand songs, until the instrument reeks with sweetness. But can a human instrument, long out of tune and sadly injured, e'er be brought back to harmony of being? In the studio of the sculptor lie blocks of deserted marble. Out of one emerges a hand, another exhibits the outlines of a face. But for some reason the artist has forsaken them. It seems that as the chisel worked inward, it uncovered some crack or revealed a dark stain. Therefore the sculptor passed it by, preferring the flawless block of snowy marble. Is the soul soiled by sin, to be cast off by the divine Sculptor?

Journeying across the plains, travelers looking through the car windows behold the California trail. The wagon ruts have become ditches, and the old route is marked by human graves. But long ago men exchanged the ox cart, the deep wagon ruts, and the wearisome journey, for palace cars. Thus there are many paths of sin worn deep by pressure of human feet. Many would fain forsake them. But is there any divine power to cast up some divine highway? Is there a happiness? Nature is kind to her grains and sweeps them forward toward harvests; is kind toward her apple seeds and bids them journey unto orchards; is kind unto the March days, and bids them journey into perpetual summer.

And man would fain find some divine friend who will lead him unto great personal worth. As if to fulfill man's deepest needs, Jesus Christ enters the earthly scene. He comes to hasten man's step along that pathway that leads from littleness unto largeness. Before our admiring vision the Divine Teacher seems like some sacred husbandman, His garden our earth, good men and great earth's richest fruit. He asks each youth to love and make the most of himself, that later on he may be bread to the hungry, medicine to the wounded, shelter to the weak. He bids each love his own reason, getting wisdom with that eager passion that Hugh Miller had for knowledge. He bids each make the most of friendship, emulating Plato in his love for his noble teacher. He asks each to love industry, emulating Peabody, whose generosity gushed like rivers. He asks each to make the most of courage and self-reliance, emulating Livingstone in self-denying service. He bids each emulate and look up to Jesus Christ, as Dante, midst the pitchy night, looked up toward the star. He bids each move heaven and earth to achieve for himself a worthy manhood. For thus only can earth ever be moved back unto heaven.

###

www.ingramcontent.com/pod-product-compliance
Lightning Source LLC
Chambersburg PA
CBHW071046290526
45795CB00004B/1345